COP to COP:

A Peer Support Training Manual
For Law Enforcement Officers
2nd Edition

Rachelle Katz, Ed.D.

Daniel I. Cohen, Ph.D.

Ronnie M. Hirsh, Ph.D.

❧ PEER SUPPORT PRESS ❦

ISBN: 0-9669496-3-3

Printed in the United States of America

January 2000

TABLE OF CONTENTS

ACKNOWLEDGEMENTS

This training manual is dedicated to the outstanding peer support officers of the Members Assistance Program (MAP) of the New York City Police Unions. Their volunteer spirit and extraordinary dedication to helping their fellow police officers is most impressive. It has been extremely gratifying to work with and train this exceptional group of men and women.

In particular, we acknowledge the dedication and commitment of three special people: Walter McCaffrey, New York City Council Member, William Genet, Director of the Members Assistance Program, and Daniel Rudofossi, Ph.D., NYPD Uniformed Psychologist and MAP liaison medical officer. Their combined efforts have literally saved lives and significantly aided hundreds of NYPD officers.

January 2000

FOREWORD

Having directed the official psychological service component of the Members Assistance Program for The New York City Police Department Medical Division, I have worked with numerous peer support officers who have shown the utmost dedication, perseverance and selfless commitment in helping fellow officers with problems. Much of the excellent work of the peer support team, such as their knowledge of the importance of setting boundaries, their noninterference with the treatment process, and their awareness of the difference between counseling and peer support, is directly attributed to the work and the professional dignity of Dr. Ronnie Hirsh, Dr. Rachelle Katz, and Dr. Daniel Cohen. The extraordinary peer support officers that they have trained have been a critical first link towards identifying fellow officers in need of mental health services.

I have personally worked with Drs. Hirsh, Katz, and Cohen. As clinicians and trainers, they have proven themselves to be assets to their profession. In addition to being personable, they are aggressive in pursuing the best standards of supervision and training for police officers of all ranks, gender, ethnic diversity and age groups. They are committed to providing police officers with the best help available.

It is for these reasons that I unequivocally recommend this training guide for any professional police-run peer support program, or to any agency dealing with law enforcement personnel.

Daniel C. Rudofossi, Ph.D., B.C.E.T.S.
Police Department - City of New York
(Retired)

INTRODUCTION

The utilization of peer support in law enforcement agencies is a relatively new development. The first official peer support training programs for officers were created in the early 1980's. These programs were intended to be preventative and to serve as early detection mechanisms to help officers deal with personal problems in their early stages.

In recent years, many law enforcement agencies around the country have begun to develop and implement peer support programs to help their officers better deal with stress and emotional difficulties. The high rates of alcoholism, domestic violence, divorce, and suicide among law enforcement personnel have made it very apparent that there are serious consequences for officers who do not reach out for the help they need. Unaddressed problems are more likely to grow to crisis proportions.

Officers generally avoid using the psychological services provided by their departments because they fear being stigmatized and disciplined as well as having career goals disrupted or destroyed. Many are also unwilling to go for help to outside mental health professionals because they believe that they will not be understood by anyone not in the law enforcement field. It is well known that officers are more willing to trust and confide in a fellow officer. They would be more likely to use a peer support officer as a sounding board to ventilate and explore problems, especially if they feel safe and know that they are not being judged. In addition, they will be more open when they believe that the information they are sharing will be kept confidential.

Peer support programs can provide a much-needed alternative in assisting officers that need help. These programs can identify a wide range of problem areas, such as depression, alcohol abuse, suicidal feelings and behavior, marital difficulties, and domestic violence. They can also identify critical incident stress, post-shooting trauma, and posttraumatic stress.

Peer support officers who are trained to recognize various symptoms and problems, and to make appropriate referrals, can have a strong impact in assisting fellow officers. A peer support team can help reduce the daily stress of law enforcement work. It can also alleviate the emotional impact of critical incidents and can prevent the buildup of anger, frustration, and despair that often leads to alcohol abuse, domestic violence, depression, and suicide.

Peer support officers (PSOs) are individuals who demonstrate good rapport with their fellow officers, good listening and interpersonal skills, sensitivity, good judgment, maturity, trustworthiness, and a genuine willingness and desire to help their co-workers. The role of a peer support officer can be stated, as follows:

1. To be available as a supportive resource for fellow officers

2. To use helping skills and concepts to assist others to explore ideas, feelings, and alternatives to situations, and to make responsible decisions

3. To evaluate and determine appropriate referrals for individuals needing professional assistance

4. To always attempt to create a safe, open, confidential, non-judgmental atmosphere within which officers can discuss their concerns

Peer support officers can be very instrumental in helping to change the law enforcement culture whereby seeking help voluntarily in addressing a personal problem can be seen as a sign of strength rather than as a weakness. PSOs serve as a first line of defense and a bridge to outside professional help when necessary. They can obtain help for their members at the earliest stage, before problems become insurmountable and jeopardize an officer's career, marriage, or life.

The Purpose of This Training Manual

This training manual has been written to teach and reinforce the skills needed to be effective as a peer support officer. It is our hope that you will read this manual thoroughly and refer to it when needed.

This manual:

1. Reviews the use of various interpersonal skills
2. Provides helpful tips
3. Discusses relevant ethical issues for PSOs
4. Provides signs and symptoms of various problem areas including alcohol abuse, relationship problems, critical incident stress, posttraumatic stress disorder, depression, and suicide
5. Provides case examples of these various problem areas
6. Offers information on stress, stress management, and self-care
7. Explains different types of psychotherapy and how to make referrals
8. Provides information on the development of a peer support program,, including an example of operational procedures

9. Answers basic questions that may come up in your role as a peer supporter

Chapter 1

ETHICAL ISSUES

As a peer support officer, you represent the program for which you have volunteered. All your behaviors and actions reflect on the credibility of the program, and it is important for you to maintain and uphold certain ethical principles and guidelines at all times. Any inappropriate behavior that you engage in will damage the trust that fellow officers place in the program. It is particularly important within the law enforcement community to be attentive to upholding these ethical standards.

There is nothing more important than your personal integrity and your respect for each individual's dignity, self-development, and personal welfare. You are expected to be a positive role model. You are someone who is expected to be truly available to help others in need. You have a responsibility to the clients you serve.

In your role as a PSO, it is imperative that you do not exercise power over others or derive personal gain from helping others. It is unethical to accept any gifts or remuneration for your work even when the client is merely being appreciative of your help. PSOs must not engage in activities that seek to meet their personal needs at the expense of the client. It is unacceptable to ask for favors or any help from clients. Your sole reward is the satisfaction of helping a troubled officer.

As a PSO, it is very important that you only offer services for which you have been trained and supervised. It is important to recognize your limitations, and that you are not a psychologist or a professional counselor. You are also not to function in the role of a union delegate or in any other advisory capacity when you are acting as a peer supporter. It is important that you maintain an exclusive role as a peer supporter when a client is receiving your help in that capacity.

In developing a healthy and helpful peer support relationship, there are certain ethical issues that need to be considered and understood.

♦ **TRUST**

In order for clients to be helped by a peer supporter, they need to trust that person. Therefore, in your initial contact you want to establish an appropriate atmosphere for **trust** to begin to develop by being open, honest, and respectful of the client.

In developing trust, it helps to explain your role and describe what services you can and cannot offer as a trained peer supporter. Trust can be damaged when a client expects more than is given. Basically, peer supporters are caring and attentive listeners, serving as a bridge to helping troubled officers find the professional help they require. Your role is not to solve the clients' problems for them. It is inappropriate for you to give advice or to tell someone what to do. By sticking to the structure of the peer supporter role, you will best maintain the trust of clients.

♦ CONFIDENTIALITY

Confidentiality means that you will respect and protect the privacy of the individual who is sharing his or her concerns with you. A law enforcement agency is a small world where rumors abound. It is important that you not discuss your clients with anyone outside the structure of your program. Officers will not reach out for help if they don't trust that complete confidentiality is maintained. It is the essential element for the success of any peer support program.

However, there may be times when you must let a client know that there are certain situations where confidentiality can and must be breached. When a client's condition indicates that there is a clear and imminent danger to the client or others, the PSO must take reasonable action to inform potential victims and/or inform responsible authorities. The first step would be to consult with your program director before taking any action. Some examples of clear and imminent danger are:

A. Child abuse
B. Potential suicide
C. Potential homicide - There is a duty to warn someone who is being overtly and directly threatened.

Since PSOs are also law enforcement officers, you have a sworn duty to enforce the law. Clients should be warned that confidentiality can and must be breached when there are indications of illegal behavior.

Fortunately, situations like the ones mentioned above are rare. In the vast majority of cases, you will be able to fully maintain client confidentiality. And, it is crucially important to reassure the client that in the vast majority of situations, confidentiality will be maintained. Confidentiality is the cornerstone of any helping relationship.

♦ <u>BOUNDARIES</u>

As a peer helper, you are in a position of some authority, and it is of utmost importance for you to not take advantage of a client's vulnerability. When you are functioning as a PSO, you have a particular role. You are a trained helper, not an "instant best friend." Keeping your role clearly in mind will help you avoid crossing the boundary lines needed for effective peer support.

When clients seek out your help they may become increasingly needy and dependent. In order not to encourage dependence:

1. It is essential that you do not become overly responsible for, or involved in, the life of the person you are trying to help.
2. Do not allow that person to become overly involved in your life.
3. Do not fall into the role of trying to rescue the individual, by doing more than is appropriate. This actually harms rather than helps the person who is seeking your assistance. The PSO approach often differs from your training as a law enforcement officer where you were trained to specifically

problem solve and rescue others. As a peer supporter, this is inappropriate.

4. Do not involve yourself in a **dual relationship** with the client where you take on a second role. This will help you avoid conflict of interest situations. For example:

   A. Do not go into business together.

   B. Do not become involved in a romantic or sexual relationship. Sexual intimacy with clients is absolutely unethical.

   C. If you find yourself getting emotionally involved with your client, remove yourself from the PSO role, and connect the individual with a different PSO. Discuss your feelings with a fellow PSO or program supervisor.

   D. Frequently PSOs have other job-related roles (such as delegate or supervisor) that can conflict with the PSO role. If you find yourself in this situation, you will need to choose one role, and refer the client to someone else to fulfill the other need. That way you will avoid potential conflicts of interest. For example, an officer may come to you and complain about being mistreated by his/her boss. As a PSO, your responsibilities are to listen and to help the person explore his/her thoughts and feelings about the situation. As a delegate, your role would be to advise the officer of options, for example, a transfer. It can be confusing and unhelpful for you to try to perform both roles simultaneously.

In summary, it is your personal qualities that will allow you to be most effective and helpful as a peer support officer. Being responsible, dependable, and trustworthy, as well as being understanding and following through on promises and commitments, will enable you to make a positive contribution to the welfare of your fellow officers.

Questions about Ethical Issues

1. What is meant by the term "dual relationship"?

_____

_____

_____

_____

2. In the role of a PSO, is it appropriate to loan money to a fellow officer client who is having financial problems? If not, why not?

_____

_____

_____

_____

3. In an attempt to help a client who is having problems with a supervisor, is it appropriate for you as a PSO to talk to his/her supervisor? If not, why not?

_____

_____

_____

_____

4. What would you do if a client called you several times a day and late at night?

_____

_____

_____

_____

5. Would it ever be appropriate to hug a client? What limits are necessary and/or appropriate?

_____

_____

_____

_____

6. Can you think of a situation when you would need to lie to a client? When might that be?

_____

_____

_____

_____

Chapter 2

INTERPERSONAL COMMUNICATION SKILLS

How one communicates as a peer support officer can make a significant difference in the quality of help that one provides to clients. Communication is complex. It can be both overt and subtle, and involves both verbal and nonverbal elements. For example, a slight grimace can make a person feel judged and criticized, thus preventing that person from sharing more information. An inflection in one's voice can signal negative feedback to the client. It is very important to be aware of <u>what</u> you are saying and <u>how</u> you are speaking to a client in order to facilitate trust, concern, and helpfulness.

Most law enforcement officers who volunteer to become peer supporters have been told that they have good communication skills, and that they are kind, sensitive, and caring individuals. You may feel you already possess all the skills required to help a fellow officer since you may have been acting unofficially in this capacity for years. The way to relate to clients as a peer support officer, however, differs from relating to family and friends. The communication style is also very different than the way you have been trained as a law enforcement officer. Please be open, therefore, to the suggestions presented in this chapter, for they can make a significant difference in improving your ability to help your peers.

Good communication exists when what is said is what is heard. Effective communication consists of three elements: 1.Mirroring, 2.Validation, and 3.Empathy

1. <u>Mirroring</u> is the process of accurately reflecting back the content of a statement. The most common form of mirroring is paraphrasing, which is stating in your own words what you are hearing. It indicates a willingness to understand the other person's point of view. For example, "What I hear you saying is..."

2. <u>Validation</u> is a communication to the other person that the information being received and mirrored makes sense and is true for that person. Validating phrases include: "I can see that..." "It makes sense to me that..." "I can understand that...." These phrases convey that the other person's subjective experience is not crazy and is a valid way of looking at things. To validate does not mean that you agree with the other person's point of view or that it reflects your own subjective experience. Mirroring and validation affirm the other person, and increase trust and closeness.

3. <u>Empathy</u> is the process of imagining the feelings the other person is experiencing, attempting to recognize and, to some extent, experience the emotions of the other person. Empathy has healing power. You might say, "I imagine that you are feeling..." or "I understand that you feel...," and checking out your guess by saying, "Is that what you are feeling?"

To help you refine your interpersonal communication skills, this chapter discusses the skills of relating, listening, and responding. Before any help can be given and accepted, it is important to establish rapport and trust with those who seek your help.

RELATING SKILLS

◆ **Putting a client at ease**

In order to relate well with others, certain conditions must exist. First, you want to put the person at ease. The client may not have ever approached anyone for help before, and may be nervous. The person may also feel concerned about opening up to you, a complete stranger, or an acquaintance that he or she barely knows. You want to make the person feel as comfortable as possible. When talking to a client on a help-line, or meeting a client for the first time, introduce yourself and provide a little information about your peer support program. One way to introduce yourself is by saying:

"Hello, my name is _____. Before we begin, I want you to know that I am a trained, volunteer peer support officer for the "Name of your peer support program". I want you to know that our discussions are confidential. Do you have any questions?"

You want to make the person feel comfortable yet you want to be careful not to dominate the conversation by speaking too much.

It is important to observe the emotional state of the client seeking your help. Look at the person, and notice non-verbal cues. Are their hands shaking or sweating? Do they seem anxious?   If you observe that the person is uncomfortable, you might ask:

"Is coming to talk to me difficult for you?"

"How are you doing right now?"

If a client is quiet, you might ask,

"What brings you here today to talk to me?"

"How can I help you?"

"What can I do for you?"

♦ **Care for your fellow officer**

You need to demonstrate to those seeking your help that you care about them, that your primary motivation for doing this work is to help, and that you respect, accept, and understand the person with whom you are working. How do you accomplish this?

Those who seek out your help may need reassurance that your motives are pure in your role as a PSO. They may not have the information that you are a good-hearted person. They may not know that your work for this peer support program is strictly voluntary and that you receive no benefits other than the satisfaction of helping other officers. Not only may they not know about your reasons for becoming a peer support officer, they may not understand the nature of your program. It may take a little time to create an atmosphere whereby a fellow officer feels comfortable opening up to you. Don't expect every client to tell you immediately what problems he or she is experiencing. Some may need to take a bit of time. It is acceptable to engage in small talk if you feel the client needs a little time before sharing his or her real issues.

Bear in mind that helping fellow officers is always for their welfare. While helping others may make you feel good, it is important that you keep your priorities clear. There may be times when you will digress and talk to a client about work, sports, movies, or other current events. This is fine as long as you don't forget your primary purpose. You must always have <u>the welfare of the other officer as your number one priority</u> as a PSO.

♦ **<u>Be Respectful</u>**

You may not always like the people who seek your help. It is not essential that you do. It is vitally important, however, that you <u>respect</u> those who ask for your help. To show respect:

1. Allow the client the right to express personal feelings, ideas, and attitudes.

2. Allow the client to make personal decisions and to find solutions to problems.

3. Respect and protect the client's privacy, by not discussing with others what the person has said. Rumors or stories may spread like wildfire. Your maintaining confidentiality is absolutely essential in order for others to feel respected by you. Law enforcement personnel, in particular, are very concerned that their issues are kept confidential, and you want to respect this need at all times.

4. Avoid jokes that poke fun at the client. Oftentimes, officers use humor to defuse stressful and painful situations. Telling jokes may be a good way to put someone at ease if they are uncomfortable. However, avoid making jokes that may be construed as offensive, such as racist or sexist jokes. Humorous comments about the other person could be interpreted as judgmental, negative, or biased. While humor may be intended as a form of teasing and meant to be benign, your best intentions may go unrecognized if the officer believes you are laughing at, or judging, his

or her feelings. Most people will not say when they find humor offensive; they will simply withdraw.

◆ Be Accepting of your fellow officer

Another condition that is essential to creating trust and rapport is your <u>acceptance</u> of the other person. In many law enforcement agencies, officers complain that they feel judged both by civilians and by the department itself. Many feel that their actions and beliefs are constantly under scrutiny. Consequently, this leads officers to feel more guarded and wary. Initially, an officer may feel that you will judge his or her feelings and actions.

Law enforcement officers are more likely to trust another member of the service than a civilian, but they may not immediately trust that you will accept their feelings and behaviors. It is important that you demonstrate that you accept the other person. This does not mean that you necessarily approve of the client's behavior. It means that you are accepting of how the client <u>feels</u> about his/her situation.

Many people are unaware of how critical and judgmental they can be. Consider how judgmental and critical you may be by truthfully answering the following questions:

1. What are your beliefs about marital infidelity? Do you see it as immoral?
2. What do you think of a person who goes bankrupt? Do you think it's irresponsible?
3. Do you have any prejudices towards any particular racial or ethnic group or towards gays or lesbians?
4. Do you see alcoholics as people who lack willpower?

No one is completely devoid of all judgements and prejudices. However, sharing your personal values does not promote open communication. It is not appropriate to express your personal beliefs and prejudices to the client to whom you are providing help. For example, if a fellow officer comes to you for help because of confused feelings as a result of having a marital affair, you do _not_ want to communicate that you believe his or her behavior is immoral and wrong. You want to help the officer by pursuing how the officer is feeling. A good way to avoid being critical and judgmental is by focusing on the person's feelings first. You might ask:

"How were you feeling when that happened?"

"How are you feeling about the experience now?"

"What was going on in your life that led to your having an affair?"

The more one truly listens to another person, the less judgmental and critical one tends to be.

♦ **<u>Be Understanding</u>**

<u>Understanding</u> a person is another important element in the development of a helping relationship. People don't expect you to have the same experiences or feelings that they do. They do want, however, to feel that you understand their needs and concerns. You can demonstrate understanding and acceptance by your verbal and non-verbal behaviors. Non-verbal behaviors include your posture, tone of voice, eye contact, facial expressions, and gestures. You may want to nod your head when you understand the feeling a client is trying to convey. You may also want to use facial expressions to convey understanding of emotions, such as sadness or fear.

Another way to show that you understand is by drawing an analogy to a similar experience you may have had. However, if you haven't had a similar experience, that is not a problem. Do not make one up to try to make the client feel understood. Honesty is very important in establishing trust. If a client discovers you made up a story, your credibility and trust will most likely be damaged.

Yet another way to demonstrate understanding is by imagining yourself in the other person's shoes, and not judging or evaluating what is being said. You might share with the client that you've thought about what your feelings would be like if you experienced a similar situation. Many people do not experience this type of understanding very often in their lives, and they tend to really appreciate it.

In helping fellow officers, you want to create an atmosphere in which they feel an openness to talk about their feelings and concerns. You want them to feel like they can trust you with their innermost emotions.

LISTENING SKILLS

Listening is a very important element in helping someone to feel better. Most people assume listening is easy but it really requires concentration and energy. It is an active skill rather than a passive one. When you are with a client, try to clear your mind of all thoughts except those that are being spoken to you by the other person. This is not always easy to do, and you may find that intrusive thoughts may creep into your mind while listening to a client. When this occurs, recognize it and quickly refocus on the client. The very least you can do is provide a client with your full attention.

A most important listening skill is good eye contact. This may contradict your training as a law enforcement officer where you may have been instructed to constantly be aware of your surroundings. You may have been taught to observe the existing conditions of a room by sitting with your back to the wall and continually having your eyes scan the environment. While this may be an effective security technique, it is not an effective communication technique as a peer support officer. The person to whom you are listening may assume you are not paying attention to his or her concerns if you are not focusing your eyes on the person.

Train yourself to keep your eyes focused exclusively on the client without appearing to stare.

Many law enforcement officers perfect a way of staring at others to assess truth and honesty. They may look at a person with a sharp, intense stare. As a PSO, you will find it more effective to <u>soften</u> your eyes so that others feel your compassion and concern. A hard stare may make fellow officers as uncomfortable as it does some perpetrators, and cause them to close down communication.

You need to listen to both the words that are spoken as well as to the tone of voice. Of equal importance to what people say is <u>how</u> they say it. Tone of voice can convey a variety of emotions like sarcasm, pessimism, hopelessness, disbelief, etc. The actual words provide certain information about what the person is trying to communicate, while the tone of voice provides additional information. Be aware that there may be a discrepancy between <u>what</u> is being said and <u>how</u> it is said. For example, a person may say, "I'm not angry," but their tone of voice suggests that they are indeed angry. How many times have you heard the expression, "The job is on the level." It may be said in a calm tone of voice yet the implication is that the person doesn't trust the job at all. Another example of a mixed message can be, "I'm all right,

I've been in shootings before." The officer may try to appear fine yet may be deeply shaken and upset by a traumatic incident. It is important to look beyond what is being said and focus on inner feelings.

It is helpful to acknowledge what is being said by, for example, nodding your head or giving a short response, like "I see," or "I understand." By doing so, you provide some feedback that you have heard the person. Now he or she can continue sharing experiences and feelings with you.

RESPONDING SKILLS

The typical ways of responding to others may not be appropriate as a peer support officer. It is natural when we speak to others in emotional distress to try to make them feel better. It is common to respond with reassuring words like, "Don't worry. Everything will be all right." While the underlying intent of those words may stem from genuine concern, the words offer little help and may be, in fact, inaccurate. Before you provide reassurance, you need to be certain that everything will actually be all right. Otherwise, it is merely a platitude, and ultimately not helpful to the person. A more helpful response might be to reflect back what you hear the person saying. For example, you can say, "That sounds like a very difficult situation for you to be going through right now." You might also say, "I can see how upsetting this is for you right now."

Similarly, it is important not to diminish a person's feelings about a situation. If someone is feeling extremely upset, avoid saying "That's no big deal." Your intent may be to provide support. However, you may be minimizing how the person feels. Individuals react very differently to situations. What may be minor to one person may be catastrophic to another. Telling someone to "lighten up" or "chill out" doesn't generally help the person to overcome negative feelings. When hearing a comment like that, many people feel misunderstood and withdraw from the help being offered.

It is quite common when we hear that a person has experienced a negative event to try providing that person with some perspective designed to make them feel better. For example, upon hearing someone was in a car accident and that his or her car was damaged, people often say, "Well, at least you weren't hurt." If someone gets robbed, they are often told, "Well, at least you weren't physically injured." While it is true that things might have been worse, these comments diminish what the person is feeling. A more appropriate response might be to ask, "How do you feel about this happening to you?" Don't assume you know how the person is feeling. Their past experience may shape their reaction to this current situation, and it may be quite different than you assume. The current situation may be opening up traumatic wounds from the past. <u>Don't make assumptions</u>. Ask how the person is feeling.

Another common unhelpful way of responding to someone who is seeking help is to analyze the situation. This stems from an attempt to explain a particular behavior.

For example, telling a person who doesn't participate in social interactions that he/she is shy and insecure may be accurate, but ultimately not helpful in providing the person with the support needed to change.

As a law enforcement officer, you may pride yourself on being a problem solver. As a peer support officer, you must avoid this role at all costs. <u>You are not responsible for solving your fellow officer's problems.</u> **YOU ARE NOT TO GIVE ADVICE**. Your responsibility is to provide support to the client and an opportunity to express concerns and feelings. Your role is to help the client identify problems and to direct that person to further help when needed.

Frequently, those asking for help speak in generalities. As a PSO, you want to utilize your responding skills to identify the more important underlying problem. Marital or relationship problems are frequent reasons why officers seek out a PSO. You may find yourself being asked for a referral to a couples therapist. Before you make a quick referral, ask some questions about what is going on in the person's life. Marital problems may be the symptom of an underlying individual problem like alcohol abuse, gambling or a personality problem. Again, you don't want to just accept things at face value. With further exploration, you can gain greater understanding of the situation and respond in the most helpful way possible.

With your responses, you want to elicit as much information and emotion from clients as possible. One way to discover more fully what the person is experiencing is to ask questions that are **open-ended** as opposed to questions that can be answered with a yes or no answer. An example of an open-ended question is "How did that experience make you feel?" or "What has been going on in your relationship?" Open-ended questions allow the person to explore and elaborate. If the client is being vague or using generalities, ask the client to be more specific.

<u>Avoid starting a question with the word "**Why**</u>." For example, when you ask a question like "Why did you do that?" people tend to give brief answers. They also tend to associate "why" questions with judgment and criticism and become defensive as a result, as they try to explain and justify their behavior. It is preferable to begin a question with the word "<u>what</u>" or "<u>how</u>." For example, "What motivated you to do that?" will tend to elicit more information, be experienced as less threatening, and better communicate your interest and desire to understand.

When in doubt about what to say to the person, ask a question that focuses on <u>feelings</u>. You cannot be expected to be a mind reader and automatically know what a person is feeling. The range of human emotions is quite broad. To highlight how varied feelings are, here is a sample of some of them:

Feelings List

Sadness	Delight
Jealousy	Grief
Anxiety	Love
Shock	Pain
Joy	Panic
Distress	Anger
Pity	Surprise
Fear	Compassion
Disappointment	Guilt
Happiness	Impatience
Frustration	Exhilaration
Affection	Boredom
Hysteria	Loneliness

When a client shares how he or she is feeling, make a statement that reflects back to the person the feelings being conveyed to you. This indicates you understand how the person is feeling and helps clarify the feelings.

After the client speaks for a while, you may respond with a comment that summarizes several statements, to put things in perspective and to determine whether you have been following accurately what has been said.

On occasion, you may utilize self-disclosure, briefly sharing some aspect of your own experience that you have in common with your client. This demonstrates your emotional understanding of the client's situation. Remember, however, that the focus is primarily on the client's experience and not your own.

Don't be afraid to make mistakes. Not even an expert in communications is a perfect communicator. If you make a mistake, apologize, redirect your response, and move on. Most people are very forgiving of conversational blunders if they recognize that your intentions are good. When someone wants help, that is their primary concern, and not how well you elicit information from them.

SUMMARY OF RESPONDING SKILLS

Remember, how you respond to a client is very important in determining how helpful you will be as a PSO.

DO NOT

- ◆ Do not reassure with pat phrases. Such words offer little help and may be inaccurate.

- ◆ Do not minimize the problems of others.

- ◆ Do not problem solve. Your responsibility as a PSO is to provide support and to allow clients to find their own solutions. Do not take responsibility for the other person's problems.

- ◆ **DO NOT GIVE ADVICE.**

- ◆ Do not assume. Ask the client for clarification.

- ◆ Do not judge.

- ◆ Do not analyze.

- ◆ Do not interpret.

♦ Do not ask questions that begin with "Why." These questions are often associated with judgement and criticism, and generally make people feel defensive.

DO

♦ Ask open-ended questions. These questions generally begin with "How" or "What" and elicit more information by allowing the client to more fully explore and elaborate their feelings and concerns.

♦ Reflect content and feelings back to the client.

♦ Summarize.

♦ Focus on feelings.

♦ Stay in the here and now.

♦ Be non-judgmental.

♦ Offer your support.

♦ Reassure the client that he or she can resolve personal problems.

- ♦ Ask for help from other PSOs and your program director when necessary.

Interpersonal Communication Questions

1. What are the main components in establishing a good <u>relationship</u> with a client?

_____

_____

_____

_____

_____

2. What are the most important ways that you can demonstrate that you are <u>listening</u> to your client?

_____

_____

_____

_____

_____

3. Name 3 "don'ts" and 3 "dos" with regard to <u>responding</u> to a client?

_____

_____

_____

_____

_____

4. Would there ever be a time when it would be appropriate to <u>interrupt</u> a client who is talking about a particular problem? When and how?

_____

_____

_____

_____

_____

5. Would it ever be helpful to a client to <u>analyze</u> or <u>interpret</u> his/her problems? What can you do instead?

_____

_____

_____

_____

_____

6. Would there ever be an appropriate time when it would be helpful to <u>reassure</u> a client that everything they are going through will turn out favorably? What alternatives do you have?

_____

_____

_____

_____

7. The following situations may be typical of what you may encounter as a PSO. Imagine putting yourself in the shoes of your clients and consider which basic human needs are underlying each situation. What questions would you ask the clients in order to help them better understand what they are experiencing?

Problem 1: A female officer, who has recently returned to work after a maternity leave, asks if she can speak to you. She tells you that she has been grumpy and irritable, and just doesn't feel like her normal self. What basic need might underlie her complaint? How might you help her explore this?

_____

_____

_____

_____

_____

_____

_____

_____

_____

Problem 2: A fellow officer tells you that he is upset that he has not been able to get any overtime. He appears anxious and agitated. What basic need might underlie his complaint? What questions would help him clarify his feelings?

_____

_____

_____

_____

_____

_____

_____

Problem 3: A newly transferred officer tells you that she feels isolated from her colleagues. She feels people are shunning her because of rumors of her past performance. What basic need might underlie her complaint? How can you help her identify possible solutions?

_____

_____

_____

_____

_____

_____

Chapter 3

PROBLEM AREAS

CONSEQUENCES OF THE STRESSES OF LAW ENFORCEMENT

Being a law enforcement officer means being exposed to many different stresses that can eventually cause serious physical and emotional problems, as well as have serious effects on personal, marital, and family relationships. There are stresses from outside of the department. These include the public's animosity and disrespect, the media's negative or distorted coverage, as well as the court's leniency to offenders and restrictions on officers. Then, there are stresses from within the department, such as offensive policies and procedures, inadequate training, lack of identity and recognition, poor economic benefits and working conditions. Other internal stresses include excessive paperwork, inconsistent discipline, favoritism, and the threat of internal investigations. Additionally, there are the stresses of the job itself. Changing schedules, having to work weekends and holidays, the constant exposure to life's miseries and brutalities, boredom mixed with the need for sudden alertness and mobilized energy, and, of course, the fear and risk of injury or death can all contribute to one's stress level.

As a result of the various work-related stresses, many officers experience personal problems and a great deal of family dysfunction, including high rates of alcoholism, domestic violence, divorce, depression, and suicide. On the job, officers become quite adept at turning off their emotions. They are taught to repress emotion, to always maintain control, take charge, be the authority, and not admit mistakes. This hardening of emotions and attitudes often makes it increasingly difficult for officers to relate to family and friends in a healthy manner. A constant barrage of difficult problems and negative situations leave many officers frustrated, drained, and emotionally depleted. Over time, some become increasingly cynical, cold, and withdrawn. In addition, many officers become over-protective, authoritarian, controlling, and restrictive with their spouses and children, who, in turn, become resentful and angry.

The following is an example of how the stressors of the job can affect officers. Officer A. is a 38-year-old woman with ten years on the job. In addition to her high-pressured job in the Department, she is going to school to complete her college degree. Divorced for more than five years, she recently began a relationship with a man who has two of his own children. She has one child, a 14-year-old boy, who is disruptive and disobedient at home and at school. All of these factors have contributed to Officer A. feeling very overwhelmed.

Officer A. has little time to give her son the attention he needs. In fact, she is so angry with him that she has withdrawn her affection from him. Consequently, he feels rejected and unloved, and is acting out even more. Officer A. feels frustrated, irritable, depressed, and guilt-ridden in addition to being anxious and worried about her own physical and emotional stability. She has been experiencing headaches, and has had difficulty falling asleep at night. She has felt on the verge of a total collapse.

Officer A. contacted a PSO with whom she was acquainted and has been directed to professional help. She is currently in therapy, and is focusing on improving her relationship with her son, and seeking ways to reduce her levels of stress.

As can be seen from this example, communication often breaks down in law enforcement families, and relationships come apart. Officers tend to confide only in other officers and not family members, in part to protect the family from the negative aspects of the job, but also because of the belief that they can only be really understood by other officers. This can create an emotional distance in law enforcement marriages and, consequently, officers experience a very high divorce rate. This is particularly true for officers in their first three years on the job, where studies have reported divorce rates as high as 70% to 80% (Kirschman, 1997). This seems to indicate that young officers and their spouses are ill-prepared for all the stresses that they soon experience, such as midnight shifts, isolation, loneliness, loss of weekends and holidays together, etc.

Another major consequence of all the stress of law enforcement work is the excessive use of alcohol. Officers are well known for using alcohol as a way to unwind after work and to bond with each other. However, many are sedating themselves, masking their feelings, and further isolating themselves from their families. In one study of officers, excessive drinkers were significantly more likely to end up divorced than those who were non-excessive drinkers (Johnson, 1991).

Yet another serious consequence of law enforcement work-related stress is domestic violence, with higher rates of physical and verbal abuse found in law enforcement families than in families in general. In one study, 40% of the officers interviewed reported having been either physically or verbally abusive to a member of their immediate family in the previous six months (Johnson, 1991).

The most tragic consequence of all is the high suicide rate of law enforcement personnel. Officers always have a gun available to them, and if they are under great stress, and using alcohol, the risk of them turning that gun on themselves during an impulsive moment of crisis increases greatly. It has also been found that marital and relationship problems are a major factor in law enforcement suicide as well. One study that demonstrates this showed that officers reporting significant marital problems were almost 5 times more likely to have attempted suicide than those not reporting significant marital problems (Janik & Kravitz, 1994). And in another study, of actual officer suicides, marital trouble was found to be the most important precipitating stress (Danto, 1978).

Helping officers improve their relationships, marriages, and family life is a very important goal. Many officers who reach out for help do so because of relationship problems. A large part of the solution to improving the lives and job performance of officers lies in finding viable methods of improving the quality of their marital and family life. Officers and family members need to be educated to be able to identify the early warning signs of maladaptation to stress. And officers need to understand the conflicts and problems that can arise from their professional activities, and the impact their work often has on their spouses, children, parents, siblings, and friends. Family members often feel isolated from officers who do not share their experiences and feelings with them. In addition, family members also experience loneliness, fear of firearms in the home, and the negative comments of neighbors who stigmatize police work.

Officers also need to understand that their professional self is not their total self, and need to experience themselves, and be experienced by people in their broader communities, as full human beings rather than just members of the law enforcement community.

HEALTHY AND UNHEALTHY RELATIONSHIPS

As a PSO, you will find that many officers will be reaching out to you for help because of relationship problems. Although you are not a professional counselor and not expected to solve relationship problems, it is important for you to have some understanding about what constitutes healthy and unhealthy relationships in order to know when to make an appropriate referral. Bear in mind that law enforcement officers are not always part of a "traditional" relationship. Some may be involved with a member of their own gender. Our comments about relationships apply to non-traditional relationships as well as traditional ones.

There are many different issues that can create problems for couples. Among the more common ones are financial pressures, conflicts and problems with extended family members, and personal differences.

To cite an actual case example, Officer B. has been married for 10 years. He and his wife have one child, a 4-year-old boy. The B.'s recently separated after a series of escalating, bitter and angry verbal fights. Officer B.'s wife could not tolerate the fights and demanded that he move out while they try to resolve their problems.

Officer B. felt disoriented and depressed, and confused about what he did wrong to create the difficulties in his marriage. He spoke to a PSO in his command and he and his wife were directed to a marital therapist. Officer B. could only tolerate a brief number of sessions, however he did gain some important perspective and understanding about his role in the breakdown of communication in his marriage.

He realized that he became more and more emotionally withdrawn from his wife as the demands of his job increased, and she, in turn, became more sexually and emotionally alienated from him. They no longer trusted each other or turned to each other for support. To make matters worse, he realized that he began to confide in, and spend more time with, his partner who happened to be a woman. While he did not have an affair with his partner, his wife became jealous and suspicious which created greater distance between them.

Officer B. recognized that he needed to reach out to his wife, and try to get closer to her if he wanted the marriage to remain intact. It is too soon to tell if his efforts at saving his marriage will be successful.

As mentioned in the previous section, the field of law enforcement tends to create additional stresses for couples. They include:

1. Irregular shifts
2. Working weekends and holidays
3. Public scrutiny
4. Over-protectiveness of family members
5. Hypervigilance
6. "Interrogating" family members
7. Being overly authoritarian
8. Presence of a gun in the home

There may be little one can do to change some of the demands of one's law enforcement job. Irregular shifts and working on weekends and holidays may be something that needs to be accepted by law enforcement couples. However, talking about one's feelings in regard to these conditions can make a big difference in the quality of one's relationship. Feeling understood, respected, and loved are generally what individuals seek from a relationship.

Sharing feelings about stressful issues can enhance these positive feelings.

Relationship problems create much emotional pain for individuals, and many want to reduce their discomfort and find ways to improve their relationships. You can encourage clients to communicate better with their partners. <u>Communication is the most important element in maintaining a healthy relationship</u>. Couples experience difficulty primarily when communication breaks down. You want to help clients recognize the value of communicating more openly with their partners.

Communication can break down when partners no longer spend time together and do enjoyable things together. Having fun with a partner is very important, as are some other positive activities. A healthy relationship needs to have a balance of more positive interactions than negative ones in order to thrive and flourish. The following are some examples of positive interactions in a relationship, and can be suggested to a client:

1. Showing interest in each other
2. Being affectionate to one another
3. Being appreciative of the efforts of a partner

4. Being supportive, empathic, and understanding to one's partner

5. Being accepting and respectful of the feelings of one's partner

6. Using humor and playfulness, and sharing pleasurable experiences with each other

7. Reintroducing praise and admiration to one's partner

8. Taking responsibility for one's behavior

9. Apologizing when one makes mistakes

If a client comes to you and complains about his or her relationship, you might ask if the couple engages in any pleasurable activities together. If the response is negative, you might ask what could they add to their relationship that would be satisfying and rewarding for both parties. The following are some tips for law enforcement families:

♦ Develop and pursue a hobby or an activity together. It can be easy to live separate lives, coming together only for chore-related matters. It's important to a relationship to have fun together.

♦ At least once a day, spend a few minutes talking. It is important to not allow any distractions, like children, television, or the phone, to interfere with this quality time with your partner.

♦ Spend at least ten minutes a day alone, either relaxing or meditating. Having a small amount of "down" time can help a person stay centered and focused.

♦ Extend your social network to include friends who are not law enforcement officers. This can provide a wider perspective on life.

♦ Don't assume you know what your partner wants or expects from you. You are not a mind reader. Check it out, by asking your partner directly.

Communication is most effective when both partners are willing to be open to the other and to fully listen to each other. You want to encourage clients to be responsive and receptive. This requires that couples avoid being critical, contemptuous, defensive, and stonewalling. These four elements are the most destructive in the breakdown of communication between couples (Gottman, 1994).

They are defined as follows:

1. <u>Being critical</u> - attacking someone's personality or character rather than a specific behavior, and usually with blame.
2. <u>Expressing contempt</u> - the intention to insult and to be psychologically abusive to one's partner by using insults, name-calling, hostile humor, mockery, and sarcasm.
3. <u>Being defensive</u> - involves denying responsibility, making excuses, and ignoring what is said.
4. <u>Stonewalling</u> - occurs when someone stops responding, withdraws, and is silent, conveying disapproval, icy distance, and smugness.

These four elements destroy love and respect, and need to be avoided by couples as much as possible. How can this be accomplished? Rather than criticizing a partner, it is preferable to complain about a <u>particular behavior</u> that is problematic. It may appear to be splitting hairs, but a complaint about a behavior is <u>specific</u>, while criticizing one's partner is more general, and more hurtful. An example of the difference between a complaint and a criticism is:

Complaint: "I'm upset you didn't ask about my day, but talked all about yours throughout dinner."

Criticism: "You show no interest in my work. You just don't care about me at all. You only care about yourself."

One way to remedy being critical is by stating grievances and complaints in a manner that will not be taken as a personal attack. This includes avoiding being contemptuous. Even though one may want to call a partner an insulting name or be sarcastic, it is preferable to control this desire. Putting one's partner down is hurtful both to the other person and the relationship, and should be avoided. Recommend to clients who tend to be critical and contemptuous that they think about what they want to communicate before they speak to their partners, to better screen out hurtful and insulting comments.

Most people become defensive when criticized. As a PSO, you can recommend to clients that instead of just trying to protect oneself and explain or justify one's behavior, it is preferable to stay calm and to listen to the feelings that one's partner is trying to communicate. It may be difficult initially to maintain control over one's reaction, but, with practice, a person can integrate these skills and enhance communication. What a person says or does not say can make a significant difference in the quality of one's relationship. It is very important to eliminate being abusive and disrespectful, and to act in as loving and respectful a manner as possible.

When a fellow officer comes to you for help with a relationship problem, remember that <u>you are not expected to solve the person's relationship problems</u>. However, you can:

- ◆ Encourage the client to talk about the problem and to explore feelings.

- ◆ Encourage the client to fight fairly with his or her partner in order to achieve a deeper and more satisfying relationship. Some rules of fair fighting are as follows:

1. **Don't fight to win**. You are allies, not enemies. In order to win, someone must lose. Fight to <u>communicate</u> rather than win. Good communication is the road to learning more about each other.

2. **Stick to the issue**. Don't take the focus off the immediate problem by straying onto other topics. Know exactly what you are fighting about. If you find the quarrel is straying, call a brief time-out, and bring it back on track.

3. **Stick to the present**. Don't bring up the past. Going over past transgressions is not productive, and creates bad feelings.

4. **Express your feelings as honestly and as fully as possible, and be considerate of the other person**. Feelings are not weapons to be used against each other; rather they should be used as information. Remember that feelings are not facts; they can and do change as your view of the situation shifts.

5. **Criticize the action, not the person**. For example, "It makes me angry when you neglect to take out the trash," as compared to, "You're such a slob; you didn't take out the trash again."

6. **Respect each other as equals**.

7. **Choose your time and place to argue constructively**. Coming home from an exhausting day at work is not the best time to have a fight. Ideally, both partners should be somewhat relaxed. Picking a specific time to argue helps to resolve issues and to avoid a power struggle.

8. **Remember that the goals of fighting are to learn about yourself and your partner, to share your thoughts and feelings with your partner, and to communicate your needs, wants, and desires**. You don't want to destroy your partner; you want to educate him or her.

9. **Listen carefully**. Be open to really listening to what your partner is trying to tell you.

10. **Don't interrupt**. Use active listening skills. If you are thinking ahead to your next comment, you are not going to hear clearly.

11. **Ideally, a quarrel should end with some resolution**. Resolutions are reached by mutual understanding, negotiation, and compromise, or by accepting that some issues must be put on hold. Even if a disagreement remains unresolved, a healthy argument leads you closer to a mutually satisfactory conclusion. Remember that you can always put the discussion back on the agenda for a later time.

In summary, as a PSO, you will have many opportunities to encourage a client to communicate more openly with, and listen more closely to, the important people in his or her life. This can help prevent the loneliness and isolation that many partners and family members experience. Better communication at home can also reduce some of the job-related attitudes and behaviors that create resentment among family members.

Remember that your role is not to solve your client's relationship problems. When you determine that there are significant problems, suggest a referral for professional relationship counseling.

Questions about Relationships

1. What are the four most destructive elements in the breakdown of communication in a relationship?

_____

_____

_____

_____

_____

2. Name 3 types of positive interactions in a relationship.

_____

_____

_____

_____

_____

3. Name 3 rules of fair fighting.

_____

_____

_____

_____

_____

4. Imagine that as a peer supporter, clients present you with the following problems. Think about what questions you might ask in order to help them, and what directions you might go in.

Problem 1: My girlfriend/boyfriend just broke up with me, and I don't know what to do. I don't think I can live without him/her.

_____

_____

_____

_____

_____

_____

Problem 2: My spouse and I have been fighting a lot lately. Last night, I almost had to hit him/her to stop him/her from yelling at me. My spouse just doesn't listen to me.

_____

_____

_____

_____

_____

_____

Problem 3: I'm married and have kids, but I'm having an affair. I think my spouse might know but hasn't said anything yet. I'm confused and tormented, and don't know what to do.

_____

_____

_____

_____

_____

_____

5. Do you believe a marriage can survive an affair? What do you imagine it would take for a marriage to survive an affair?

_____

_____

_____

_____

_____

_____

_____

ALCOHOL ABUSE
AND OTHER
COMPULSIVE BEHAVIORS

As a PSO, it is important for you to be able to identify the signs and symptoms of various compulsive behaviors. With all compulsive behaviors, it is important for you as a peer supporter to be sensitive, compassionate, and non-judgmental. Most people who suffer from compulsive disorders are highly sensitive to being judged and criticized and will withdraw if they sense you are judging them. The following are considered compulsive behaviors:

♦ **Alcohol Abuse.**

Many officers relieve stress by using alcohol. The use of alcohol is an integral part of the law enforcement culture. Social drinking may be an enjoyable way to unwind after a hard day of work. For many, however, drinking behavior escalates and becomes a problem.

Officer C. is 32 years old, and has been on the job for 12 years. He felt burnt out from so many years on patrol, and from the accumulation of miseries that he observed and has had to professionally handle. He is separated from his wife of 5 years and their young son. She told him that she is fed up with him, and will divorce him and move with her son to a far-away state.

Officer C. felt angry and frustrated a great deal of the time. He was also anxious and depressed and was averaging only four hours of sleep per night. He was drinking more and more alcohol, and going out more frequently with his officer friends to forget his troubles.

His friends told him that he seemed distracted and preoccupied. They were concerned about his impulsive behavior. When confronted with examples of some of his actions, he claimed he didn't know what they were talking about, and didn't remember the events they cited, such as getting into a fight or picking up a prostitute. He adamantly stated that he can handle alcohol and that he doesn't have a problem with it. However, he recently was in a car accident while driving alone. Luckily, he was not seriously hurt. He attributed passing out in the car to prescription medication, and claimed that alcohol had nothing to do with the accident.

Officer C. finally asked one of his friends for help, and was directed to a PSO. The PSO provided him with two referrals, one to an outpatient alcohol treatment facility and the other to an individual therapist. Officer C. went to both, and after several sessions, he acknowledged his substance abuse problem and stopped drinking alcohol. He also began attending Alcoholics Anonymous meetings.

Alcohol abuse is also a major factor in the majority of incidents of domestic violence and in most law enforcement suicides.

Some Facts About Alcoholism

- Heavy and chronic drinking:
    - Can harm virtually every organ and system in the body.
    - Is the most important cause of illness and death from liver disease.
    - Is associated with cardiovascular diseases such as hypertension and stroke.
    - Contributes to approximately 65% of all cases of pancreatitis.
    - Depresses the immune system and results in a predisposition to infectious diseases, including respiratory infections, pneumonia, and tuberculosis.
- Nearly 13.8 million Americans have problems with alcohol.

- Alcoholism contributes to 100,000 deaths annually, making it the third leading cause of preventable mortality in the U.S.

- Studies of suicide victims in the general population show that about 20% are alcoholic.

- 40% of all traffic fatalities are alcohol-related. Alcoholics are nearly five times more likely than others to die in car crashes.

- About 43% of Americans, 76 million people, have been exposed to alcoholism in the family.

- Nearly one-fourth of all persons admitted to general hospitals have alcohol problems or are undiagnosed alcoholics being treated for the consequences of their drinking.

- Separated and divorced men and women were three times as likely as married men and women to say they had been married to an alcoholic or problem drinker.

♦ An estimated 6.6 million children under the age of 18 live in households with at least one alcoholic parent.

♦ Children of alcoholics are 4 times more likely to become alcoholics than children of non-alcoholic parents.

For most people, alcohol is a pleasant accompaniment while socializing. Moderate alcohol use, defined as two drinks per day for men and one drink per day for women and older people, is not considered harmful for most people. A substantial number of people, however, have serious problems with drinking. Almost 14 million Americans, 1 in every 13 adults, abuse alcohol or are alcoholic. Several million more adults engage in a risky drinking pattern that could lead to alcohol problems.

What is alcoholism? Alcoholism is a disease that is characterized by the following elements:

❖ **Craving**: A strong need or compulsion to drink.
❖ **Loss of control**: The inability to stop drinking once a person has begun.

- ❖ **Physical dependence**: Physical withdrawal symptoms, such as nausea, sweating, shakiness, and anxiety when alcohol is stopped after heavy drinking.
- ❖ **Tolerance**: The need to consume increasing amounts of alcohol to experience the same "high."

Many people wonder why some individuals can use alcohol without problems while others are unable to control the amount they drink. Recent research suggests that many people have a genetic predisposition to becoming alcoholic. Alcoholism is inherited like other diseases, such as diabetes and cancer. Yet it is also important to recognize that aspects of a person's environment are significant influences as well.

Much of our knowledge about alcoholism has been gathered from research conducted with men. However, some recent studies have included women. These studies reveal that differences exist between men and women with regard to drinking. As a peer support officer, it is important to be aware that female clients may have particular problems and needs in regard to excessive alcohol consumption.

In the general American population, fewer women than men drink. Of the estimated 14 million alcohol-abusing or alcohol-dependent individuals, approximately 4.6 million are women. Women become more intoxicated than men when drinking identical amounts of alcohol. Some reasons for this are:

1. Women have less water in their bodies than men, so the alcohol is less diluted and has greater impact;
2. Women do not metabolize alcohol as efficiently as men because they may not have a stomach enzyme that helps digest alcohol;
3. Hormonal levels from a woman's menstrual cycle may effect how intoxicated a woman becomes.

Research suggests that women may be at higher risk for developing alcohol-related problems at lower levels of consumption than men. Female alcoholics have death rates 50 to 100 % higher than male alcoholics. Furthermore, a greater percentage of female alcoholics die from suicides, alcohol-related accidents, cirrhosis, and hepatitis. Problem drinking also has adverse effects on fertility and sexual function. The frequency of menstrual disturbances, spontaneous abortions, and miscarriages increases with increased levels of drinking. The death rate from breast cancer was 30% higher among middle-aged and elderly women who reported drinking at least one drink daily as compared to non-drinkers.

A recent study linked victimization to alcohol problems. Of all the alcoholic women in the study, 90% were physically or sexually abused as children. Alcohol and other drug usage make women more vulnerable to being raped. A survey of college students found that 53% of rape victims had used alcohol and/or drugs prior to being raped, while 64% of the rapists reported alcohol or other drug usage before committing the offense. Alcohol is present in more than one half of all incidents of domestic violence with women most likely to be battered when both partners have been drinking.

Women represent 25% of alcoholism clients in traditional treatment centers in the U.S. Female alcoholics may encounter different motivators and barriers to seeking treatment than men. For instance, women are more likely to seek treatment because of family problems, and are often encouraged by parents or children to seek help. Men are usually encouraged by wives to seek treatment. Fewer women than men reach treatment through the criminal justice system or through employee assistance programs.

Lack of childcare is one of the most frequently cited barriers for women seeking treatment.

Alcoholism is a disease that compromises a person's physical and emotional well being as well as the ability to function optimally at work and in interpersonal relationships. A good definition for alcohol abuse is <u>any drinking behavior that is associated with dysfunction in a person's life.</u>

Alcohol abuse has warning signs.

Some of them are:

1. Using alcohol to deal with problems
2. Having to drink more and more to get the same high
3. Hiding how much you drink
4. Forgetting things when you drink
5. Getting angry when someone complains about your drinking
6. Having trouble stopping after the first drink

When you meet with a client ask some basic questions about the person's drinking history. It is common that many problem drinkers will initially deny that they have a problem with alcohol and will claim they can stop drinking whenever they want to. Asking some detailed questions about a person's consumption of alcohol will help you determine if a problem exists and requires treatment. Ask the following questions:

1. Do you drink alcohol?
2. How much do you drink?
3. How often do you drink?
4. Have you ever experienced blackouts? (Blackouts are periods of time when a person is unable to recall what has happened.)
5. Has there ever been a time in your life when you wished you didn't drink?

The following is another set of questions that can help a client decide if he or she has an alcohol problem. To help you remember these four questions, remember the word **CAGE**, an acronym of the first letter of each key word in each question.

1. Have you ever felt you should **Cut down** your drinking?
2. Have people **Annoyed** you by criticizing your drinking?
3. Have you ever felt bad or **Guilty** about your drinking?

4. Have you ever had a drink first thing in the morning to steady your nerves or to get rid of a hangover (**Eye opener**)?

Alcoholism is a treatable disease. If you determine that the client has an alcohol problem, a referral for treatment is necessary. Treatment may include detoxification in an inpatient facility or an outpatient alcohol treatment facility. These facilities generally provide individual and group counseling as well. The involvement of family members may be important to the recovery process and brief marital or family therapy may also be part of the treatment.

Alcoholism affects everyone in the family. For the recovery process to be successful, family members and colleagues generally must change the way they relate to the alcoholic person. A pattern may have developed whereby a spouse, children, and/or co-workers have **enabled** the alcoholic to continue drinking by shielding him or her from the negative consequences of the excessive drinking. For instance, a spouse may enable by making excuses for the alcoholic, by saying he or she is ill rather than hung-over. Some other examples of enabling behavior are:

1. Denial of an alcohol problem in one's partner

2. Justifying drinking alcohol as acceptable given the stress level of one's partner

3. Avoiding conflict with the alcoholic and not expressing one's true feelings

4. Minimizing the situation with the alcoholic as "not that bad"

5. Over-functioning by taking on the responsibilities of the alcoholic in addition to one's own

6. Being controlling

7. Being a martyr

8. Treating the alcoholic partner as a child

9. Passively waiting for things to improve

Family members and work colleagues that are enablers need to change their behavior once an alcoholic enters recovery for the sake of the alcoholic as well as for themselves. Enabling behaviors perpetuate the alcoholic's problems and negatively affect everyone else in close proximity.

A most effective support system for alcoholics is Alcoholics Anonymous (AA), a world wide fellowship of men and women who help each other stay sober by utilizing a 12 -Step program for recovery. As a PSO, you can volunteer to accompany an officer to an open meeting if that helps the client get over some initial resistance to going. AA meetings are often an important step in changing the direction of an alcoholic's life. In addition, there is also Al-Anon, which holds meetings for family members and friends of alcoholics.

Alcoholism is considered a compulsive disorder. Compulsive disorders are often the result of attempts to deal with the negative aspects of stress. There are other behaviors that are compulsive in nature that are sometimes even more hidden than alcohol abuse. The following are examples:

◆ Steroid Abuse

We live in a culture where superficial characteristics, like physical attractiveness, are prized. Cultural messages affect everyone to some extent. This can include law enforcement officers as well. Many officers practice a regular schedule of weight training in order to maintain superior physical strength and muscle definition. Carried to an extreme, the desire for a muscular body can lead to an obsession where the individual begins to utilize steroid drugs to enhance physical abilities. Steroid abusers can suffer from a wide range of side effects. Some physical effects are:

1. Hardening of the arteries

2. Acne

3. Sterility

4. Impotence

Some psychological effects arc:

1. Aggressive or combative behavior known as "roid rage"

2. Irritability and moodiness

If a client seems extremely irritable and moody, you may want to question whether or not that person is using steroids. Be aware that withdrawal from steroids can cause extreme depression and should be monitored by a physician.

♦ Eating Disorders

Eating disorders are an extreme expression of weight and food issues. They include anorexia nervosa (self-starvation), bulimia (binge/purge syndrome), and compulsive overeating.

Literally, anorexia nervosa means loss of appetite, but this is a misnomer. Anorexics are hungry. They will deny their hunger because of an irrational fear of becoming fat. Anorexia is characterized by self-starvation, preoccupation with food and rituals, excessive exercising, and for women, the loss of one's monthly menstruation.

Bulimia is characterized by periods of binge eating, consuming large quantities of food in a short period of time, followed by purging, either through vomiting, abuse of laxatives or diuretics, or periods of fasting. While the weight of most bulimics is within the normal range, their weight can fluctuate during a binge.

A compulsive overeater or binge eater eats what others would consider an abnormally large amount of food. Binge eaters frequently feel they are unable to control the amount of food they consume. Usually, compulsive overeaters become overweight.

Symptoms of any compulsive behavior can recur following a traumatic incident. A female police officer, Officer D., was involved in an off-duty car accident that caused cuts and bruises to her face. She needed stitches to close the wounds. She felt disfigured from the stitches, and was deeply disturbed by this since looks were very important to her family. This accident triggered a relapse in binge eating and vomiting, compulsive behaviors that she experienced as a teenage girl.

While she would not divulge her bulimic behavior with a peer support officer, she did tell her that she was very upset and could not stop crying. She was referred to a psychotherapist. Upon evaluation, it was determined that her binge eating and purging were occurring so frequently that she needed to be treated in an in-patient facility. She stayed there for 28 days, and then continued weekly psychotherapy to deal with her depression and anxiety.

Another female officer, Officer E., also binged and purged, which was followed by days of fasting. She had experienced several incidents of sexual abuse as a child and felt tremendous shame as a result of these experiences. She was trying to cleanse herself from these negative feelings. She recognized that her behavior was out-of-control.

She knew of the peer support program from a flyer at her command, called the help-line, met with a peer supporter, and was referred to a psychotherapist. She attended weekly psychotherapy sessions that helped her regain control of her eating behavior. Psychotherapy helped her to make the commitment to stop binging and purging as well as fasting, and to overcome the self-loathing she experienced. Each day was a struggle to eat in a healthy and nutritious way, yet she was very successful in changing her lifestyle.

All eating disorders can be serious and may have life-threatening consequences. These behaviors arise from feelings of inadequacy, depression, anxiety, and loneliness, as well as troubled family and personal relationships. Dieting, binge eating, and purging initially help some people cope with painful emotions and feel as if they are in control of their lives. Yet at the same time, these behaviors undermine health, self-esteem, and a sense of competence and control.

Psychotherapy and attending a 12 -Step support program, such as Overeaters Anonymous, is generally necessary to help a person with an eating disorder change this self-destructive behavior.

♦ Compulsive Gambling

Compulsive gambling is another behavior that can be utilized in an attempt to reduce stress. This behavior usually progresses from occasional gambling to habitual gambling. The urge to gamble becomes so great that only more gambling can relieve the tension. Like other addictions, compulsive gambling alters the chemistry of the brain by elevating dopamine levels. The increase in dopamine creates a pleasurable sensation and fuels a physical and psychological desire to continue the behavior.

As the person continues to gamble, it takes more and more of the behavior to produce the same effect. Higher stakes and personal risks become involved, as well as neglect of other interests, family, and work. Severe family problems, financial ruin, and criminal behavior to support the gambling habit may result.

As legalized gambling has blossomed from a blip in the U.S. economy to a $500 billion a year industry, compulsive gambling has greatly increased as well. Experts now estimate that slightly more than 5% of the U.S. population has a moderate or severe problem with gambling. Fortunately, help is available for people who struggle with compulsive gambling. Just as the 12-Step program of AA has been so helpful for the recovery of alcoholics, Gamblers Anonymous (GA), also a 12-Step program, forms the core of recovery for compulsive gamblers. Similar to AA, GA members share their experiences in group meetings with peers who desire to stop gambling.

◆ **Debting and Overspending**

Related to gambling is debting and overspending. Some of the features are:

1. Compulsive spending
2. Impulsive purchases

3. Living beyond one's means

4. Credit card debt

5. Bankruptcy

A person may compulsively purchase items to distract himself/herself from feelings of depression and anxiety.

The following is an example of an officer with multiple compulsive behaviors, one of which is debting and overspending. Officer F. is a single, 31-year-old male, who still lives with his parents. He explains that this is simply a way to save money on rent, however, he doesn't see himself as capable of taking care of himself. He doesn't cook, clean or attend to any other basic household activities. He spends many hours watching television and eating junk food. He is overweight and sees himself as unattractive. Although he has made attempts to develop relationships with women, they all ended as a result of his being unfaithful. He spends most of his money on pornography, which further isolates him and interferes with his ability to be intimate with girlfriends. The amount of money he spends on pornography and junk food prevents him from pursuing healthier hobbies and activities.

Officer F. has very low self-esteem and sees himself in a very negative light. He feels that he is not good enough and is undeserving of love and affection. He expresses a desire to break out of his unhealthy patterns, but feels stuck in these behaviors. He did meet with a psychotherapist for several sessions, based on the recommendation of a peer support officer, but did not feel ready to commit to the process and did not continue further treatment.

◆ **Sexual Addiction**

This disorder is defined as sexual behaviors with increasingly harmful consequences and the participant's inability to discontinue them. Some of the harmful consequences are:

1. Loss of important relationships
2. Physical diseases
3. Possible arrest for sexual crimes
4. Depression or anxiety that may result from shame, secrecy, and lowered self-esteem

The following is an example of an officer with a sexual addiction problem. Officer G. is a 39-year-old man whose second marriage is on the rocks. He is an intense, outgoing, talkative person, who has a long-term problem with intimacy, commitment, and faithfulness. He has had numerous affairs during both of his marriages. He can also be characterized as anxious, insecure, and impulsive.

Although he feels guilty over his affairs, he seems unable to control his need to have sexual encounters with numerous women. He is puzzled by his behavior, but does have some awareness that he is trying to "prove" himself in some way. However, he blames his wife for turning away from him. He denies having affairs to her, but she does not believe him, and wants out of their marriage. She has told him that she does not trust him nor does she feel emotionally safe with him. She feels that he has been dominating and controlling with her, jealous and suspicious, "interrogating" her at every turn.

Officer G. spoke to a friend who happens to be the peer support officer in his command. He was directed to a psychotherapist, and continues to work on his emotional and relationship issues.

In all addictions, addicts employ typical defenses of denial, rationalization, justification, and minimization in order to continue the behavior. Treatment must break through these defenses to help someone recover. As a peer supporter, you may encounter clients who initially deny they have a problem or claim that they can stop at any time. You may therefore need to exercise patience before a client is ready to admit to a problem and seek help.

Substance Abuse Questions

1. Define alcoholism?

_____

_____

_____

_____

_____

2. What does **CAGE** stand for?

_____

_____

_____

_____

3. What is a blackout? Do social drinkers experience blackouts?

_____

_____

_____

_____

_____

4. What is the primary defense mechanism utilized by alcoholics?

_____

_____

_____

_____

_____

5. As a PSO, what questions might you ask a client who is denying that he/she is having a problem with alcohol?

_____

_____

_____

_____

_____

_____

6. As a PSO, what might you tell a client who shares with you that his/her parents were both alcoholics?

_____

_____

_____

_____

7. What warning signs might you look for to detect an individual with an alcohol problem?

_____

_____

_____

_____

_____

_____

8. What are some of the side effects for an individual who is abusing steroids?

_____

_____

_____

_____

_____

9. What are the 3 main eating disorders and what are some characteristics of each?

_____

_____

_____

_____

10.   What signs might you look for to detect a compulsive
      gambler?   What are some of the consequences of this
      behavior?

_____

_____

_____

_____

_____

_____

11.   What signs might you look for to detect an individual
      with a sexual compulsion?   What are some of the
      consequences of sexual compulsions?

_____

_____

_____

_____

_____

_____

12. If you told a client with a compulsive disorder to just stop the behavior, do you think that person would be able to? What can help people to stop compulsive behaviors?

_____

_____

_____

_____

_____

_____

DEPRESSION

Depression is a mood disorder that occurs in varying intensities and can be experienced in different ways. For most people, depression is just a bad mood that may last for a day or two. For some, however, depression is a debilitating chronic illness. Depression becomes a significant problem when it begins to interfere with one's physical health, job performance, and personal and family relationships. Depression is one of the most widespread emotional disorders. When severe, depression is a major factor in many, if not most, suicides.

A "normal" depressed mood occurs typically when one experiences losses, such as the breakup of a relationship or marriage, the death of a close relative or friend, a failure at work or school, or a sudden rejection. As peer supporters, you will generally be talking with fellow officers who are depressed as a reaction to such traumatic life events. In many, if not most, instances, you will be referring depressed individuals to a mental health professional for further evaluation, therapy, and, possibly, medication.

In order to be able to recognize depression, you need to know its signs and symptoms. There are four categories of depressive symptoms: physical, emotional, cognitive, and behavioral.

♦ **Physical symptoms**

1. Changes in eating patterns - Although some depressed people may experience an increase in appetite and a weight gain, most have a poor appetite, a lack of interest in food, and a weight loss that can be rapid and alarming.

2. Changes in sleeping patterns - The depressed person might have difficulty falling asleep (insomnia), may sleep irregularly, may awaken early in the morning before wanting to, or occasionally may not be able to get out of bed at all.

3. Low energy or fatigue - This is the most common complaint of depressed individuals.

4. Loss of interest in sex - This may include temporary impotence.

5. Backaches, headaches, upset stomach, and constipation

♦ **Emotional symptoms**

1. Sadness, often accompanied by crying, and usually experienced most intensely in the

morning - This is the most common emotional symptom of depressed individuals.

2. Feeling helpless, hopeless, and unhappy

3. Feeling worthless, useless, lonely, and empty

4. Feeling excessive or inappropriate guilt and shame

5. Feeling anxious, or agitated - This may be accompanied by pacing, moaning, and hand wringing.

6. Experiencing little or no pleasure or gratification from interests, activities, and relationships that previously brought satisfaction - Work, hobbies, recreational activities, and close friends no longer seem exciting or interesting.

♦ **Cognitive symptoms**

These are the perceptions and thoughts that accompany depression. The depressed person often has:

1. A negative self-image, low self-esteem, and feelings of inadequacy or incompetence

2. An exaggerated experience of past failures or disappointments, often accompanied by self-blame and guilt

3. Pessimistic thoughts about the future, recurrent thoughts of death, suicidal thoughts, or a suicidal plan - Time passes slowly and the world seems dreary and meaningless.

♦ **Behavioral symptoms**

These are the changes in a depressed person's behavior. Depressed people are often:

1.   Passive, having little motivation to initiate any kind of activity - This includes a general withdrawal from human contact.

2.   Unable to maintain good grooming habits - In more severe cases, routine tasks, like changing clothes, are even difficult to accomplish.

3.   Lethargic, and walk, speak, and react slowly- This often includes toneless speech and an expressionless face.

4.   Indecisive and have poor concentration - Decisions are often overwhelming and frightening to make, and depressed people avoid problem-solving tasks.

The following is a case example of a person who suffers from depression. Officer H. is a 35-year-old male with 10 years on the job. He is unhappy, lonely, and isolated. He sleeps most of the time that he is not at work, binge eats, and has low energy. Physically, he is overweight and experiences various physical symptoms. He feels as if a dark cloud hangs over his life.

Officer H. comes from a highly dysfunctional family. His parents divorced when he was a small child. He doesn't feel anybody has ever really been there for him. He feels that people have disappointed him countless times. He has difficulty experiencing any pleasure, even from activities that he used to enjoy. He has no thoughts of suicide, but keeps thinking about past disappointments and is quite pessimistic about the future. He is becoming more and more withdrawn from others, and feels like a social outcast.

Officer H. called the Peer Support Help-line, spoke to and then met with a peer support officer. The PSO recognized Officer H.'s symptoms of depression and referred him to a psychotherapist. He is currently in treatment with a psychologist for his depression.

Depression must be taken seriously. It is often the precursor of suicide. As a PSO, it is important to recognize the signs of depression in order to direct the client to professional help. With depressed clients in particular, you need to strongly encourage the client to be evaluated professionally. Follow up frequently until you are satisfied that the client is getting proper care.

Questions about Depression

1. What are the four categories of depressive symptoms? List one symptom from each category?

_____

_____

_____

_____

_____

2. As a PSO, what would you do if a client meets with you and starts to cry?

_____

_____

_____

_____

3. As a PSO, what would you do if a client meets with you and does not talk?

_____

_____

_____

_____

4. What are some helpful comments you might say to a depressed client?

_____

_____

_____

_____

_____

5. What is your primary objective in dealing with a client who is suffering from depression?

_____

_____

_____

_____

_____

_____

_____

CRITICAL INCIDENT STRESS (CIS)

A critical incident is any incident that causes emergency service personnel to experience unusually strong emotional and physical reactions that have the potential to interfere with their ability to function normally at work and/or in their personal lives. It is very common and quite normal for people to experience emotional aftershocks following a traumatic event.

Critical incident stress is a person's response to a specific traumatic event that is of such intensity and magnitude that it overwhelms the individual's normal coping skills. Critical incident stress can create considerable psychological and physiological discomfort and symptoms for the person. These symptoms can appear immediately after the traumatic event, within the first hours or days, or, in some cases, weeks and months may pass before stress symptoms appear. Remember that two individuals at the same incident may have very different reactions.

Most law enforcement officers (approximately 85%) exposed to a traumatic event experience stress symptoms to some degree. If an officer receives understanding and support, the stress reactions usually pass more quickly.

The following is an example of two undercover officers who experienced a critical incident. Officer I. and Officer J.were robbed of their guns and radios by a perpetrator. The perpetrator handcuffed them to a pole. To become free, they had to ask a civilian to call 911. After the incident, they were questioned separately for several hours by supervisors. Their delegate asked them how they were feeling and if they thought they would like to see a psychotherapist. Both agreed. On the following day, they met with a psychotherapist together for an hour, and then each met separately with the therapist once a week for several months to discuss their individual feelings.

Officer I. felt guilty that he did not do more to stop the perpetrator, and questioned his competence as a police officer. Coming from a family of law enforcement officers, he felt he did not live up to the standard of his father and uncles. He was uncomfortable about going back to work. It took him a couple of months before he felt capable of returning to work to resume his former duties.

Officer J. felt vulnerable after the incident and uncomfortable being out of his house. He began to experience trouble sleeping and had panic attacks. He began to withdraw from his family and friends. He thought he was going crazy. He, too, did not feel comfortable returning to work, and it took several months before he was ready to be placed on active duty.

As a law enforcement officer, you are quite familiar with the types of critical situations that officers experience. As a PSO:

♦ Reassure a client who has experienced a critical incident that his/her reactions are normal under the circumstances, and are not crazy. Providing reassurance in this kind of situation is very helpful. Emphasize that it is much healthier to deal openly and directly with his/her feelings than to repress them.

♦ Encourage the officer to talk about what happened, in as much detail as possible, and what he/she was feeling. Allow the person to ventilate what he/she is feeling currently. Encourage the expression of any emotion, whether it is anger, regret, sadness, guilt, fear, etc. Be careful not to take the client's anger or other feelings personally.

◆ Refer the officer to a Critical Incident Stress Debriefing (CISD), if available. CISD is a group meeting or discussion for individuals who participated in a specific traumatic event. It is held by specially trained individuals and always includes a specially trained mental health professional as part of the team. It is designed to lessen the psychological impact of a traumatic event and to prevent the subsequent development of more serious symptoms. It also serves as an early identification mechanism for individuals who may need professional help to resolve their reactions.

When critical incident stress is dealt with quickly, longer-term traumatic stress effects can be prevented and the affected officer can be restored to normal functioning within a reasonable period of time. In your role as PSOs, you can have a very significant effect on the recovery of officers from these critical events. When critical stress reactions are hidden and unresolved, and emotions are not adequately dealt with in a timely manner, recovery is hindered and posttraumatic stress disorder may later occur.

Critical Incident Stress Questions

1. What is CISD?

_____

_____

_____

_____

_____

_____

2. Can you talk to a client too soon after the occurrence of a critical incident? Is it possible that a client may not immediately experience any emotions about the traumatic event? What might you say and do then?

_____

_____

_____

_____

_____

_____

_____

3. As a PSO, what helpful comments can you say to a client who just experienced a traumatic event?

_____

_____

_____

_____

_____

_____

4. Do you think it's possible for you as a PSO to feel stressed yourself after talking to a client who just went through a traumatic event? If yes, what might help you to deal with these feelings?

_____

_____

_____

_____

_____

_____

5. What qualifications are needed for conducting a debriefing?

_____

_____

_____

POSTTRAUMATIC STRESS DISORDER (PTSD)

If critical incident stress is not addressed at the time that an incident occurs, either through formal or informal means, it is more likely for an officer to develop posttraumatic stress disorder (PTSD). PTSD is an anxiety disorder produced by an uncommon, extremely stressful life event that is outside the range of usual human experience. The event producing this syndrome would be markedly distressing to almost anyone, and is usually experienced with intense fear, terror, and helplessness. The symptoms that develop following such an event can occur even months or years after the event, and usually cause significant impairment with regard to job performance, family relationships, and social functioning.

As a PSO, you will encounter PTSD primarily with regard to officers involved in shootings, serious line of duty injuries or deaths, the suicide of a fellow officer, the traumatic death of children, or a hostage situation. Officers who are experiencing CIS or PTSD will exhibit many of the following symptoms:

Physical Symptoms

♦ Headaches

♦ Muscle aches

♦ Sleep disturbances (difficulty falling or staying asleep)

♦ Changes in appetite (usually a lack of appetite)

♦ Fatigue and low energy

♦ Intense nervous system activity (such as an adrenaline rush, profuse sweating, rapid heartbeat)

♦ Nausea and dizziness

♦ Decreased interest in sexual activity (sometimes impotence, which is usually only temporary)

Emotional Symptoms

♦ Denial and avoidance of feelings associated with the trauma

♦ Feeling emotionally numb and being unable to express feelings

♦ Anxiety (such as panic attacks, fear, worry, and guilt)

♦ Depression (such as sadness, grief, crying, sense of despair, and hopelessness)

♦ Anger (such as irritability and resentment)

♦ Feeling overwhelmed and out-of-control (fear of insanity)

- Hypersensitivity and wide mood swings
- Hypervigilance (being on edge, overly alert, easily startled)

Cognitive Symptoms

- Involuntarily re-experiencing the traumatic event through flashbacks, nightmares, recurring thoughts, and intrusive memories
- Confusion and slowed thinking
- Disorientation and poor concentration
- Memory lapses
- Difficulty making decisions and solving problems
- Feeling "scattered" and unable to focus on work or daily activities
- Time distortion

Behavioral Symptoms

- Avoidance (withdrawal, isolating, diminished interest and participation in activities)
- Suspiciousness and over-protectiveness of loved ones
- Explosive outbursts (usually unprovoked)
- Poor impulse control (This can lead to an increase in alcohol consumption as an attempt to self-medicate and blunt emotions. This also makes the

person an increased risk for suicide and/or violence against others.)

The following is an example of an officer with PTSD. Officer K. is a 51-year-old male detective, with 21 years on the job. He is also a military veteran of two wars, Viet Nam and the Persian Gulf War. Ever since his service in the Persian Gulf War, he has been experiencing symptoms of PTSD. He has had flashbacks, intrusive thoughts, and distressing nightmares. He also has headaches, dizziness and gastro-intestinal problems. He does not have much of an appetite and does not sleep well.

Additionally, he is depressed, anxious, worried, and irritable. He feels detached from people, and experiences a lack of pleasure from activities that he used to enjoy. These symptoms are affecting his relationships and causing him problems at work. His marriage has disintegrated and his wife is divorcing him. His children feel alienated from him. At work, he is experiencing a great deal of difficulty performing his job as a crime scene detective. Bloody crime scenes trigger flashbacks of his wartime experiences.

Officer K. met with a peer support officer in his command, who recognized his need for both medical and psychological assistance. The PSO encouraged the officer to pursue all the treatment necessary to help him feel better. Officer K. was grateful to finally receive help for his problems.

A person with PTSD is experiencing extremes: either numbed detachment or intrusive reliving of the trauma, either hypersensitivity or insensitivity, either responding too intensely or not at all. It is helpful to tell someone experiencing PTSD that he/she is experiencing <u>a normal reaction to an abnormal situation.</u> As a PSO, when you encounter a fellow officer with PTSD, a referral for professional assistance is generally required.

You may wonder how therapy is helpful for someone suffering from PTSD. Individuals with PTSD frequently feel like they are going crazy because they don't feel that they have any control over their emotions or their physical functions. Their behavior can be so out of the ordinary from what it is normally, that they find this very disturbing. Therapy can <u>provide reassurance</u> that the person is not going crazy, that what is being experienced is completely normal relative to the trauma they have experienced. By explaining the range of symptoms, a therapist can help a person appreciate the extent and severity of the experience, and know that these symptoms are common for those who have experienced a traumatic event.

Another goal of therapy is <u>to provide support</u>. While it is important for a person with PTSD to express feelings in therapy, it is equally important for the therapist to maintain some limits so that the person does not lose control.

Another function of therapy is to help individuals <u>reduce avoidance</u>. Avoidance can occur in a number of ways. A person can try to avoid dealing with the traumatic event, and this prevents the person from healing and moving on. Avoidance limits the quality of one's life. For instance, if a person has been bitten by a dog and traumatized by this event, he or she may avoid going to people's homes where there are pets. If an officer has been traumatized by an incident where a person has been shot and killed, the officer may develop a fear of guns and avoid carrying one. Therapy can help an officer become more comfortable carrying a weapon again. If that is not possible, therapy can help an officer make a decision about his job based on a rational discussion rather than on unconscious avoidance.

The way a person feels about a traumatic experience is extremely important. One of the goals of therapy is to alter the meaning given to a traumatic event or to <u>reframe the way a person looks at the event</u>.

Therapy utilizes several techniques to help individuals overcome PTSD.

1. <u>Education</u> about stress and symptoms is an important component.

2. Teaching different forms of <u>relaxation exercises</u> can help when a person is flooded with anxiety.

3. Another useful technique is <u>positive imagery</u>. This teaches the person to imagine pleasant images to replace or reduce intrusive thoughts when they occur.

4. <u>Systematic desensitization</u> is a process that gradually allows the person to experience diminished anxiety to a traumatic event.

5. Practicing <u>coping skills</u> is another element of therapy to help someone get back on their feet.

As a PSO, you are in the position to encourage the client to utilize professional mental health care. Sharing your knowledge about PTSD with the client will have a positive effect on the individual. A professional mental health practitioner should evaluate anyone who presents with symptoms of PTSD.

Posttraumatic Stress Disorder Questions

1. Imagine that the following clients come to you for help. What kinds of help would you provide?

Problem 1: An officer was recently injured chasing an armed robber. He needed to be hospitalized for a few days because of some minor physical injuries. The officer calls to speak to you and complains that he is experiencing mood swings. The officer found that he laughed while family and friends visited, but would cry when alone. Additionally, the officer is most disturbed by being unable to concentrate, and finding that he is not able to read the incident report. The officer is afraid to tell anyone because he fears he is losing his mind. What symptoms of PTSD is the client experiencing? What help would you provide?

_____

_____

_____

_____

_____

_____

_____

Problem 2: An emotionally disturbed person attacked an officer, slashing her with a razor on her throat, arms, and back. She was unable to defend herself, and was finally helped by civilians. She asked to talk to a peer support officer because she was unable to sleep. She would fall asleep, but be awakened by nightmares of the incident. What symptoms of PTSD is she experiencing? How would you help her?

_____

_____

_____

_____

_____

_____

_____

_____

_____

_____

_____

_____

Problem 3: A detective with the crime scene unit approaches you and tells you that he is no longer comfortable doing his job. Most especially, he gets upset when collecting blood samples. Additionally, he keeps having recurring thoughts of the different crime scenes he has worked on. He doesn't discuss his work with his family, and doesn't feel close to them. He realizes that something is wrong because he is angry all the time, and feels like a volcano about to explode. What are his symptoms? How would you help him?

_____

_____

_____

_____

_____

_____

_____

_____

2. Identify two ways that therapy is helpful for someone with PTSD.

_____

_____

_____

_____

_____

3. Name two therapy techniques used to help an individual overcome PTSD.

_____

_____

_____

_____

_____

_____

4. Think of the most stressful experience you have had as an officer. What symptoms of CIS and PTSD did you experience?   In what ways did you deal with your symptoms?

_____

_____

_____

_____

_____

_____

_____

_____

GRIEF AND BEREAVEMENT

Loss is a natural part of life, and often occurs through the deaths of family members, friends, coworkers, and even pets. Other losses include changing partners at work, the end of a relationship, a divorce, or the moving away of a close neighbor. Loss can also occur within oneself, like the loss of one's youth or health. When loss occurs, it often is accompanied by strong emotions.

Grief is a natural response to loss and death, and involves deep sorrow and emotional pain. It is a process that takes time to overcome, through feeling and facing the pain of the loss. The grieving process can be divided into four stages: shock, anger, depression, and finally, acceptance and healing. Each individual experiences grief differently. Some individuals may go through the stages sequentially while others may experience them in a different order or not experience all of the stages.

The first stage of grief is shock. A sudden death generally leaves one in shock, feeling numb, detached, and helpless. Many people report that they feel like they're in a dream state. Suddenly, life no longer feels real. There is often an initial denial that the death has actually occurred.

Even though individuals have been told or know that their beloved is dead, they may have a hard time believing and accepting that it is true. Frequently, people have the sensation that the deceased is on vacation and will be coming back soon.

Crying is a natural reaction during this initial stage. It is a way to relieve tension and stress, and to express one's sadness. While many people cry during this stage, others may not be able to until some time later when the shock wears off. There can also be a variety of unusual physical sensations and symptoms associated with shock, such as muscular tightness, upset stomach, shortness of breath, and a general lethargy. Some people report that they feel the deceased person's presence in the room with them.

When the numbness wears off, the grieving person is often flooded with powerful emotions and a deep feeling of loss. Individuals may experience feelings of intense sadness, fear, guilt, and anger. These emotions need to be released and expressed as fully as possible. This is the second stage of the grieving process.

A strong emotion that survivors have difficulty acknowledging and often feel guilty about is anger. One focus of the anger can be toward the deceased, for leaving them. Survivors often feel rejected, deserted, abandoned, and overwhelmed by responsibilities. Anger may also be directed at oneself, at God, and at others. It is important for survivors to be able to express their anger, as well as their other feelings, without being judged for it. It is a very important part of the catharsis of normal grief. It is much healthier to let these feelings come out rather than to keep them locked inside.

Often survivors feel somehow responsible for their loved one's death, and begin to feel guilt and self-blame. There may be guilt over past arguments, and over not having done more for the deceased. There is often a preoccupation with the death and loss being experienced, as well as dreams and flashbacks about the loved one.

The third stage of the grieving process is depression, which can last for months. It is not uncommon for a person to become depressed when the reality of the loved one's death really sinks in. Nor is it uncommon for the loved one to contemplate his or her own death, so that as a PSO, being alert to any suicidal thoughts or feelings during grieving is extremely important. Survivors often feel very fatigued during this period.

The fourth stage of the grieving process is acceptance and healing. Dealing with the pain of a major loss in one's life helps one to move on. There is no specific time frame in getting through the mourning process. For some, it can take a matter of months, while for others, it can take years. Most people, however, are able to cope and carry on with their lives, after going through various difficult emotions. They are then able to form new relationships and pursue new interests. A few are not as successful in moving on, and may need further help, such as professional counseling or therapy, in order to more fully resolve their grief.

For example, several months after the death of his teenage son in a car accident, Officer L. became increasingly more attracted to a female officer in his precinct, and began having an affair with her. When she rejected him, he became distraught. Although he claimed he did not love her, and did not want to leave his wife, he could not stop thinking about her. He could not concentrate at work, felt restless, argued with family members and coworkers, and snapped at minor frustrations. He confided his feelings to a peer support officer in his command that referred him to a psychotherapist.

In psychotherapy he realized that he displaced his feelings of sorrow over the death of his son by acting out sexually. By focusing on his emotional pain, he was able to feel better and cope more effectively.

Oftentimes, individuals feel uncomfortable around a person who is grieving. They don't know what to say to the person or how to provide comfort and support. As a peer supporter, you may be in the position to say a few comforting words to a grieving client. If you can't think of anything to say, you can simply reflect back to the person what you believe the person is feeling. For example, you can say, "I can see you are very sad over your loss." Your presence alone can be a great comfort. You might ask if there is anything you can do to help the person. They might begin talking as a way to vent some of the feelings they are experiencing. If a grieving client wishes to talk, encourage him/her. Just listen. Don't try to change how the person feels. With a grieving client, as with all clients, it is very important to accept the client's feelings and to encourage further expression of these feelings.

Grieving individuals frequently complain about feeling distracted and having trouble concentrating. This is natural. If a client complains about being preoccupied and forgetful, you might want to reassure him or her that this is a natural response to grieving, is temporary, and will pass in due time as the individual expresses and resolves his or her feelings of grief and loss.

Questions about Grief and Bereavement

1. Name the four stages of the grieving process.

_____

_____

_____

_____

_____

_____

2. What do you think is most beneficial in helping someone who is grieving?

_____

_____

_____

_____

_____

_____

3. Examine your own history. Can you recall a time when you suffered a loss? What was it like for you to go through the grief process?

_____

_____

_____

_____

_____

_____

_____

_____

_____

Chapter 4

PREVENTING SUICIDE

Suicide among law enforcement officers has been on a dramatic upward trend in recent years. It is a major problem and has been occurring at approximately four times the suicide rate of the general population. More officers kill themselves than are killed in the line of duty.

The extreme stresses of the job, the constant barrage of situations fraught with danger, the continuous exposure to death and injury, and the regular access to a gun put officers at a much higher risk for suicide. The additional factors of shift work, alcohol abuse, family and relationship problems, depression, and financial pressures can significantly contribute to increasing a person's stress level. Alcohol abuse, in particular, has been found to be a major factor in law enforcement suicides. Suicidal risk, consequently, can grow enormously if an already stressed officer is using alcohol.

Research, in regard to law enforcement officer suicides, indicates that frustration is a particularly important factor. Individuals generally enter law enforcement work with an idealistic attitude, but after some time on the job tend to become increasingly cynical. This frustration and cynicism result from law enforcement agency bureaucracy as well as from several societal situations, like a negative public image and press, a lack of community support, and problems within the criminal justice system. Officers begin to feel isolated from society, and have difficulty asking for help. As frustrations build, and feelings of helplessness to change these factors occur, some officers reach a breaking point and begin to see suicide as an option.

Suicide is an act of desperation and an attempt to deal with feelings of frustration, helplessness, and emotional pain. It is an attempt to regain control over one's environment when one feels out of control and other options seem unavailable. Various stressful situations or major life changes and losses can trigger suicidal feelings. For law enforcement officers, these especially include critical incidents, such as shootings, line of duty injuries or deaths, and suicides of fellow officers. More general situations include:

1. death of a loved one or close friend
2. a serious illness
3. a divorce or breakup of a significant relationship
4. a failure or a financial setback
5. depression or other psychiatric disorders
6. alcohol or drug abuse
7. unemployment

8. retirement

9. the absence of a support system

You may wonder what to look for in a potentially suicidal person. <u>Be alert to changes in a person's personality or behavior.</u> These include:

1. increased sadness, withdrawal, or irritability

2. difficulty concentrating

3. loss of appetite and weight, or overeating and weight gain

4. oversleeping, insomnia, or early wakening

5. loss of interest in people and activities previously enjoyed

6. worry about money or illness

7. fears of losing control or going crazy

8. feeling worthless and hopeless

9. feeling guilt, shame, or self-hatred

10. increased drug or alcohol use

11. depression that disappears and is replaced by a sense of calm

12. giving away important possessions

Why do people use suicide as a means of ending their lives? Possible <u>motives</u> for suicides are:

1. manipulation

2. revenge

3. misdirected anger

4. distorted reality

5. not seeing any alternatives - Most suicides occur for this reason. The person does not know how else to deal with his/her painful life situation, and does not feel that it is possible to change his/her life.

Most suicidal gestures or attempts are a cry for help. <u>Any threat to commit suicide must be taken seriously.</u> As a PSO, if you believe a person is thinking about suicide, do not hesitate to ask if that is so, and if the person has a plan. By asking the question, you are not planting the idea. A suicidal person is already thinking that way. Bringing it out in the open and talking about it generally <u>reduces</u> the urgency to take such a drastic action, and makes suicide <u>less</u> likely.

For example, Officer M. is a 25-year-old male with only 3 years on the job. He felt depressed and discouraged. He was in debt, and extremely worried about his finances. He was also overweight and had several medical problems. To escape from his problems, he would drink alcohol alone at home.

His parents divorced when he was young. He had a volatile relationship with his mother, who was an alcoholic. He father disappeared from his life after the divorce. He often felt taken advantage of by friends and family, and became so distrustful of others that he withdrew and became more isolated. He felt pessimistic about the future, and could not see any way out of his various problems. He believed that if he were to die, nobody would miss him.

After a lonely night at home, Officer M. approached a peer support officer with whom he was acquainted, and asked to speak to her. As he related his problems and feelings to her, she became concerned about the possibility of his being suicidal. She utilized her training, and asked the important question: "Are you thinking about hurting yourself?" He said that he was. After further discussion, she contacted the director of the Peer Support Team, who, in turn, called a psychologist affiliated with the program. An appointment for the officer was secured within 2 hours, and the PSO accompanied the officer to his first session. Through therapy, he was able to resolve his problems, and was no longer depressed and suicidal.

When assessing a person's suicide potential, it is important to determine how much thought a person has given to a suicide attempt and whether his/her immediate environment contains specific tools of suicide. Ask the following questions:

1. Is the person thinking about suicide?
2. Has the person attempted suicide previously?
3. Has the person developed a plan?
4. Are there means available, such as a gun, pills, etc?
5. Is the person intoxicated with alcohol or drugs?
6. Is the person alone?

After asking these questions, you want to:

♦ Gather information about the person's support system. (Are there any family members or friends that this individual trusts? Is there a psychotherapist or counselor that this person is seeing or has seen?)

♦ Let the person know that you take him/her seriously.

♦ Attempt to build trust and rapport, and encourage the venting of emotions. (If the person is angry, be aware that it is not about you and do not take it personally.)

- Validate the person's feelings of hurt, anger, and pain as real.

- Attempt to reduce the lethality of the situation by, for example, removing the gun if one is present, or removing pills that may be available.

- Offer realistic hope, support, and encouragement, and attempt to reinterpret the situation in a more positive manner.

- Assure the person that he/she has worth and value.

- Generate alternatives and options concerning how to change the person's situation and feelings.

- Tell the person that further help is available.

- Make a no-suicide contract where the individual promises not to harm him/herself.

- If available, call a friend or relative of the individual to come and spend the night.

- **DO NOT LEAVE THE PERSON ALONE**.

- Make a referral to a mental health professional, and secure a specific appointment.

- Follow up the next day to see that the appointment has been carried out and to reinforce the steps the individual has already taken for him/herself.

A suicide attempt is a momentary, impulsive action generally taken during a particularly stressful period, and if you can help the individual through the crisis, a suicide can be averted.

In summary, here is a memory device for assessing suicidal risk that is called **PLAID PALS**, where each letter stands for one element of the assessment, as follows:

Plan	Is there a plan?
Lethality	Is it lethal?
Availability	Are the means available?
Illness	Is there a mental or physical illness?
Depression	Is the person depressed?
Previous	How many? How recent?
Alone	Is the person alone?
Loss	Has the person suffered a loss?
Substance abuse	Is the person using alcohol or drugs?

As a PSO, you may encounter an officer client who has lost a colleague, family member, or friend to suicide. It is important to understand that the grief process for a survivor of suicide is more difficult than the normal grief process. Survivors of suicide often search for answers that can never be found. The normal grief reaction includes denial, shock, guilt, anger, and depression. Death by suicide intensifies all these, and may also include feelings of shame, failure, and rejection. Law enforcement suicides in particular can be devastating to the morale of an entire command, and can produce intense feelings of guilt, sadness, and discouragement in officers. Allow such clients to explore their feelings as fully as possible. When appropriate, refer to a mental health professional.

Questions about Preventing Suicide

1. Identify three situations that can trigger suicidal feelings.

_____

_____

_____

_____

_____

_____

2. What are some of the personality and behavioral changes
   to be alert to with regard to suicide?

_____

_____

_____

_____

_____

_____

3. What does **PLAID PALS** stand for?

_____

_____

_____

4. Are you a religious person? How do your religious beliefs affect the way you think about suicide? Is it wise to ever tell a client that suicide is immoral?

_____

_____

_____

_____

_____

_____

_____

5. What helpful comments might you say to a client who is expressing suicidal thoughts?

_____

_____

_____

_____

_____

_____

_____

6. If a client promises you that he/she will not commit suicide, would you believe that person? What would help you believe that the person is sincere?

_____

_____

_____

_____

_____

_____

7. What risk factors make a person more likely to commit suicide?

_____

_____

_____

_____

_____

_____

_____

8. Do you know anyone who died by suicide? How did you feel? Describe the way you experienced the grief process.

_____

_____

_____

_____

_____

_____

_____

_____

_____

_____

Chapter 5

STRESS MANAGEMENT

What is **stress**? Stress is the "wear and tear" we experience as we adjust to our continually changing environment. Stress has both physical and emotional effects, and can create positive or negative feelings. As a <u>positive</u> influence, stress can help compel us to action. It can result in new awareness and an exciting new perspective. As a <u>negative</u> influence, it can lead to health problems, such as headaches, upset stomach, rashes, insomnia, ulcers, and high blood pressure. Stress can also lead to depression or anxiety.

How can you tell if someone is experiencing stress? There are some specific signs and symptoms of stress to look for. Some of the signs are physiological in nature, while others are reflected in our feelings and behaviors. Some of the signs can be obvious to others, like sweating and foot tapping, while other reactions are undetectable to others. Only the person experiencing the stress is aware of the reaction. For example, it is difficult, if not impossible, for anyone to notice your heart pounding or that you are having troublesome thoughts that will not go away.

Many of the signs of stress are subtle, but observable. If you take time to learn them, and train yourself to pay attention to them, you will be better able to recognize stress in your colleagues, and help them feel better. One of the simple keys in identifying stress is to notice <u>change</u>. Are you or the person with whom you are working acting differently from what is typical? Rather than looking for change in general, it is preferable to look for <u>specific</u> changes, like the ones listed below.

CUES TO IDENTIFY STRESS

<u>Physiological Responses</u>

- ❖ Vague physical complaints
- ❖ Sweaty palms

- ❖ Stooped posture
- ❖ Trembling
- ❖ Changes in sleep patterns

- ❖ Chronic fatigue

- ❖ Body motions (such as excessive foot tapping)
- ❖ Weight gain or loss
- ❖ Dilated pupils

Emotions

- Sadness
- Daydreaming
- Frequent mood changes

- Anger
- Being easily distractible

Behaviors

- Explosive outbursts
- Complaining
- Impulsive Actions
- Cynical or hostile remarks
- Being self-critical
- Being overly critical of others

- Talking about past more than future
- Being insubordinate to superiors
- Change in job productivity
- Increased use of alcohol, drugs, tobacco, or caffeine
- Lack of attention to details
- Being withdrawn

People are thinking beings. As we live our every day lives, we continuously think about what we do. We have expectations about the outcomes of daily events. We have concerns, beliefs, judgments, and attitudes about what we are doing. Consequently, we say things to ourselves. Called inner speech or self-statements, these thoughts can be negative or positive, and they can greatly affect our stress levels.

Albert Ellis, a cognitive psychologist, has theorized that it isn't an event itself that causes stress. It is the way an individual <u>thinks</u> about the event that creates stress. What is important about this premise is that by changing the way you think, your level of stress can diminish and you can feel more positive. You don't need to do anything differently; all you need to change are your thoughts. Increased positive self-talk, as opposed to negative, can make a profound difference in how people feel about themselves.

Imagine that you are asked to speak to a large group of citizens regarding the stress involved in your job. If you think to yourself, "I'm no good at giving talks" , chances are that stepping in front of such a group will be a frightening experience. Your prejudgment regarding your capability will significantly affect your reaction to the event. By contrast, if you say to yourself, "I don't have much experience giving talks in front of strangers, so this will be a new experience for me, and possibly help me to grow in a new way," you probably will feel much more positive about the experience.

Here is another example of the difference between positive and negative self-talk. A supervisor criticizes two employees for not performing a specific part of their job well. These two individuals may react very differently to the criticism depending on the types of self-statements they make to themselves. One might say, "Oh well, I made a mistake this time. Live and learn. I won't do it again," and feel ok about himself. The other employee might say, "I'm no good at this job. I'll never be able to get the approval of my supervisor. I'm never going to get ahead," and feel very badly about himself. These two individuals think very differently about themselves. The first one has much higher self-esteem. Additionally, their self-statements are likely to affect how they actually perform their jobs in the future. The second employee may undergo considerable anxiety trying to please the supervisor.

After making repeated negative self-statements, one is likely to develop generalized beliefs about oneself that are not accurate but leave one feeling discouraged and defeated. Negative self-talk also produces substantial uncomfortable physiological arousal where one's body becomes tense and stressed. Negative self-statements can be categorized as follows:

1. **Overgeneralization**. Rather than confining thoughts and feelings to the specific situation, the person generalizes to other things. Common words utilized in over-generalized self-statements include <u>always</u>, <u>never</u>, and <u>forever</u>. An example of an overgeneralization would be: "This always happens to me."

2. **Catastrophizing**. The person frequently thinks the worst will happen. Rather than viewing a stressful situation as unpleasant, the person sees it as a tragedy. Some examples of common words used in catastrophizing include <u>horrible</u>, <u>incredibly awful</u>, and <u>tragic</u>. "My life is ruined" is an example of a catastrophizing self-statement.

3. **Self-Pressure**. The person thinks that he or she has not lived up to some standard. Instead of thinking about what one wants, the person thinks about how things **should** be. Common self-pressuring words are "should" and "must." "I should have known better" is an example.

4. **Black or White thinking**. The person emphasizes the extremes of situations while ignoring the middle ground. Situations are either all good or all bad. An example of black or white thinking is, "All people are greedy."

5. **Blaming**. Blaming occurs when a person seeks to place blame on someone or something else when an unpleasant situation has occurred. An example would be, "It's your fault we had this car accident."

Another way to categorize negative self-statements is by the following stress-building beliefs:

1. Perfectionism

Do you feel constant pressure to achieve?

Do you feel you haven't done enough no matter how hard you try?

2. Control

Do you worry about how you appear to others when you are nervous?

Do you feel that any lack of control is a sign of weakness or failure?

3. People pleasing

Does your self-esteem depend on everyone else's opinion of you?

Are you better at caring for others than for yourself?

Do you keep most negative feelings inside to avoid displeasing others?

4. Competency

Do you feel you can never do as good a job as other people?

Do you feel you lack common sense?

Do you think you are stupid?

Stress-building statements can be modified to reduce stress, allowing the person to feel better. Two examples of the difference between a stress builder and a stress buster are:

Stress Builder: "I'll never get this project done in time."
Stress Buster: "If I stay focused, and take it one step at a time, I'll make steady progress."

Stress Builder: "I can't believe I forgot to pay the electric bill on time. If I keep this up, I'll ruin our credit."
Stress Buster: "No one is perfect. I forgot to pay the bill this time. I usually pay bills on time. I just need to pay more attention."

Certain thoughts can help <u>prevent</u> painful emotions or help to <u>reduce</u> them. Below are some examples of <u>positive self-statements</u> that can help a person deal with difficult situations.

Preparing for a stressful event

"I'm going to do the best I can."

"I'm going to be all right."

"It will only be for a few hours. I can manage."

"Stay positive. Don't let negative thoughts creep into my consciousness."

Confronting the stressful situation

"Stay organized."

"Keep focused."

"I'm doing my best."

"It's ok to make mistakes."

Coping with fear

"Try to relax."

"Just breathe deeply."

"This will end shortly."

"Let me stay active. It will reduce my fear."

Reinforcing success

"I did it."

"It's over. I survived."

"Problems don't have to get the best of me."

"I'm getting healthier and stronger."

Another important way of reducing stress is by building **physical** reserves:

- Exercise for cardiovascular fitness three or four times a week. (Moderate, prolonged rhythmic exercise is best, such as walking, swimming, cycling, or jogging.)
- Eat well-balanced nutritional meals.
- Maintain an ideal weight.
- Avoid nicotine, excessive caffeine, and other stimulants.
- Mix leisure with work.
- Take breaks.
- Get enough sleep.
- Be as consistent with your sleep schedule as possible.

The following are several techniques to help you and your clients reduce stress.

THREE MENTAL TECHNIQUES FOR STRESS MANAGEMENT

1. Modify your self-statements. Be observant of the messages you give yourself.

2. Keep a perspective on the situation. Ask yourself, "Is it really so important?"

3. Use humor and exaggeration to deflect stress.

THREE PHYSICAL TECHNIQUES FOR STRESS MANAGEMENT

1. Shoulder scrunch: move your shoulders up toward your ears and hold for a count of five. Then let go. Repeat three times.

2. Clenched fist: clench both your fists and toes and hold for a count of five. Then let go. Repeat four times.

3. Breathing technique: inhale deeply three times holding the third breath. Count to five and exhale

slowly.   Breathe in through the nose and out through the mouth. Repeat this sequence twice.

SELF-CARE

Volunteering as a PSO places you at increased risk to experience stress and burnout as a result of dealing with clients in crisis. Burnout is a syndrome of emotional exhaustion that can occur when working as a helper with people who are troubled or having serious problems (Maslach, 1982). Another name for this is "compassion fatigue." It is helpful and important to try to keep some emotional distance between yourself and the officers you are helping. This does not mean that you cease to genuinely care about them. It means that you become able to maintain what is called a "detached concern," which helps to reduce the strain and the risk of burnout.

After dealing with one or more stressful situations, and to avoid feeling drained and used up, consider the following:

1. It is imperative that you talk to your team coordinator to debrief and to discuss how you are feeling.
2. It is also a good idea to talk to other PSOs as a way to release some of the feelings you may have experienced, to "blow off some steam."

3. If necessary, you may need to take a few days off from PSO responsibilities to help you regroup. Decompress by focusing on some pleasurable and relaxing activities.

4. Helping others in crisis can trigger memories of painful experiences you may have had. At some point, you may want to talk to a mental health professional to work through any unresolved issues that you still find troubling.

5. In general, try not to overdo it by taking on more than you can handle. You are part of a team. Utilize each other. If you are not taking care of yourself, it is very hard to help someone else.

Questions about Stress Management

1. Are some individuals more nervous and stressed than others? How might you detect when someone is going through an unusually stressful and upsetting time? List several signs and symptoms of stress.

_____

_____

_____

_____

_____

_____

2. Name two categories of negative self-statements.

_____

_____

_____

_____

_____

_____

3. If you notice that a client frequently is making negative self-statements, what helpful comments might you make?

_____

_____

_____

_____

_____

_____

_____

_____

4. If a client tells you that he/she wants to do healthier activities, what might you say as a PSO to encourage such a change in that person's behavior?

_____

_____

_____

_____

_____

_____

5. **Modifying Your Inner Voice**

Please take a few moments and think about your inner conversation. What kinds of statements do you say to yourself? List three negative self-statements:

1. _____

2. _____

3. ._____

How often do you think you say these things to yourself?

    a) Several times a day

    b) Once a day

    c) Once a week

    d) Rarely

Rephrase the negative self-statements above to be more positive.

1. _____

2. _____

3. _____

Chapter 6

HOW TO MAKE REFERRALS

In your work as a PSO, a number of the officers with whom you will meet will be sufficiently helped by your interventions that they will not need any further assistance beyond the contacts they will have with you. They will only need to vent their feelings, explore their situations, and experience the kind of acceptance, support, and empathy that you are being trained to provide.

However, a certain number of your officer clients will need further assistance once you have helped them to identify their problems. A very important aspect of your PSO role is to serve as a bridge to getting them the additional help that they need by referring them appropriately. For this you need to be familiar with the kinds of organizations and people in the community to whom you can refer.

Primary sources available to you are the many self-help support groups and 12-Step programs that have developed in recent years. Alcoholics Anonymous, Al-Anon (for family members and friends of alcoholics), Gamblers Anonymous, and Overeaters Anonymous are just a few of the groups that exist which focus on a single problem area. These groups provide many people with the support and encouragement that they need in order to begin to overcome these difficult problems.

Although these self-help groups are of enormous help and importance to many people, they may not be sufficient by themselves and you may need to recommend them in conjunction with professional help. This may be in the form of a treatment center for a specific problem, such as alcoholism, other addictions, or eating disorders. However, most of the time, the referrals will be to individual mental health clinicians when you encounter officers with significant emotional problems. These include anxiety attacks, depression, chronic irritability, unresolved grief, suicidal thoughts and behavior, critical incident stress, posttraumatic stress disorder, or significant relationship, marital or family problems.

There are a number of different types of qualified mental health professionals or psychotherapists:

1. **Psychologists** have a doctorate degree, either a Ph.D. or Psy.D. in Clinical or Counseling Psychology or an Ed.D. in Counseling or Educational Psychology, and are licensed by passing a state written exam.

2. **Psychiatrists** are Medical Doctors (M.D.) with specialized training in psychiatry following medical school. They are the only psychotherapists who can prescribe medication. They are also the only ones who can hospitalize an officer should that become necessary.

3. **Clinical Social Workers** have a Masters Degree (M.S.W. or C.S.W.) plus supervised clinical experience and become accredited by passing a written national exam. If a social worker has national accreditation, he or she will also have ACSW after his or her name.

4. **Marriage and Family Therapists** hold a doctorate or masters degree in Family Therapy or other mental health field with specialized training and supervision in marriage and family therapy. An accreditation to look for is clinical membership in the American Association for Marriage and Family Therapy (AAMFT).

5. **Mental Health Counselors** have a Ph.D. or M.A. in counseling or related mental health field and are licensed in some states. An accreditation to look

for is certification by the American Counseling Association, which grants a CCMHC (Certified Clinical Mental Health Counselor) or NCC (National Certified Counselor).

6. **Masters level therapists** have graduate degrees in a specialized field, for example, addiction counseling, grief counseling. Again, look for CCMHC or NCC certification.

7. **Certified Alcohol Counselors (CAC)** have completed class-work in substance abuse counseling and an internship in a treatment facility for alcohol abuse.

There are four main ways in which psychotherapy is structured:

1. **Individual therapy** involves the therapist and client in a one-to-one encounter. Sessions are generally held once a week for 45 to 50 minutes.

2. **Couples therapy** is for relationship difficulties, pre-marital counseling, marriage counseling, and even divorce counseling. The

therapist acts as a neutral sounding board for a couple's conflicts and complaints, and helps the couple to develop better communication skills and conflict resolution techniques.

3. **Family therapy** works with the relationships primarily between parents and children where all family members can express their feelings, explore family roles, and resolve family problems.

4. **Group therapy** offers an opportunity to improve interpersonal skills and build a support network in addition to helping resolve individual emotional problems and unproductive behavior patterns.

There are many different theoretical orientations that psychotherapists may utilize. However, more important than their theoretical approach are the qualities of the individual therapist, such as compassion, warmth, good listening and relating skills, a supportive attitude, and personal integrity. And as a PSO, you want to utilize individual clinicians and facilities that have experience with, and an understanding of, the kinds of issues and problems that law enforcement officers tend to experience. Law enforcement officers and their families have special needs when it comes to mental health services. It is highly recommended and most beneficial if your peer support program is able to compile a computerized database of a provider referral network comprised of mental health clinicians familiar with these specific needs.

In deciding which category of clinician to refer a client to, consider the following as a guide:

A. When you believe that an individual is experiencing signs of serious mental illness and may need medication, the appropriate referral is to a psychiatrist.

B. When you identify alcohol as the primary underlying problem, refer to either an alcohol treatment center or to a clinician who is experienced working with alcohol abuse and recovery issues, and who is familiar with the 12-Step approach.

C. When the primary problem appears to be marital, relationship, or family issues, an appropriate referral is to a marriage and family therapist.

D. For more general emotional issues, such as low self-esteem, anxiety, stress, depression, social isolation, and career concerns, a referral to an individual therapist is appropriate.

When referring an officer for psychotherapy, you want to emphasize and reinforce that seeking help when one needs it is a sign of strength and courage and not an indication of weakness or that one is crazy. You also want to convey that professional counseling can help the client feel better and can resolve problems before a more serious crisis occurs.

When referring, consider the following:

♦ Check with the referral source to be certain that your client can be accepted for help.

♦ Discuss with your client your reason for making the referral.

♦ Help your client secure the necessary appointment.

♦ Be available to accompany your client to a support group meeting or to a clinician's appointment if that will help him/her better accept the referral. It is also a way to demonstrate that you really care about, and are committed to helping, the person.

♦ Follow up afterwards to see how your client made out as a result of the referral. By doing so, you will reinforce both the progress the client has made, as well as the client's commitment to continue to get help. You will also learn valuable information about your referral sources, and be better able to decide which ones you will want to utilize again in the future. Follow up is an essential part of your role as a PSO.

By directing your clients to the appropriate professional assistance in a timely manner, you can help these officers learn how to better cope with all of the occupational stresses and personal and relationship problems that are generally associated with law enforcement work.

Questions about Referrals

1. What do you think are the most important qualities for a therapist to possess to be able to help a fellow officer?

_____

_____

_____

_____

_____

_____

2. Do you think it is appropriate for you as a PSO to talk to a therapist to whom you are referring a client? What would you want to share?

_____

_____

_____

_____

_____

_____

3. To what kind of clinician would you refer a client who you believe is severely depressed? Explain your rationale.

_____

_____

_____

_____

_____

_____

4. Name two actions that are important for you as a PSO to take when making a referral?

_____

_____

_____

_____

_____

_____

5. Why is it important to follow up after a referral?

_____

_____

_____

_____

Chapter 7

DEVELOPING A PEER SUPPORT PROGRAM

Presented in this chapter are some ideas for the development of a peer support program. Different types of programs exist. The model presented here is one where trained peers are available on a 24-hour basis to act as the initial contact when a fellow officer needs help. Getting help is strictly voluntary. An officer is never pressured or forced into receiving peer support services. This distinguishes a peer support program from departmental programs that can require officers to participate against their will.

In this model, peer support officers do **not** provide counseling services. Although there is a tendency for peer supporters to want to do more, they are not sufficiently trained to be professional counselors. Their function is to serve as peer supporters to those who reach out for help, being available to listen, understand, and provide referrals for professional assistance when necessary.

When developing a peer support program, it is important to consider how the program will operate, and under whose auspices. It is preferable for the program to be independent of, but supported by its law enforcement agency. In this way, the program is autonomous, and able to maintain confidentiality for its participants. In most instances, the agency need not be informed when one of its members is seeking help.

The program may be developed from within the union. However, it is important for the program to ultimately be autonomous from the union as well as the department in order that participants trust that confidentiality will be maintained. Some unions may even be able to fund a peer support program. If not, federal or municipal grants may be available to help finance the development of a program.

To develop a peer support program, the first task is to have a mandate that defines the parameters of its goals, responsibilities, and limits. What exactly is the objective of the program? What types of services will it provide? Will it provide help only to officers or will it provide help to their family members as well? It is helpful for the mandate to include procedures that address what happens when officers need to be placed on leave and/or need to have their weapons temporarily safeguarded. How will the agency be involved? When these types of questions are addressed, and policies are clearly established, misunderstandings are less likely to occur. Forming a committee may be helpful to address these concerns. The committee can be comprised of members from both the union and the department.

It is also helpful for the program to be clear that when an officer is already in trouble with the department, the peer support program cannot be used to avert disciplinary action. This keeps the division of responsibilities clear between the program and the agency, avoids potential conflict with the department, and keeps officers from attempting to manipulate the program.

The second task of beginning a peer support program is to choose a director who will coordinate and run the program. The director has a very important function. He must to be able to negotiate and coordinate the necessary arrangements between the agency and the union. He needs to be a person who gets along well with others, and manages people well. Since peers are not being paid for their time and work, the director of the program must maintain good morale and a high level of enthusiasm. The director must ultimately be the person in charge. In large departments, PSOs may be divided into geographic teams, each with a team coordinator. The director would then oversee and supervise the coordinators.

The financial costs of setting up a voluntary peer support program are variable. The main expense is in the hiring of clinician/trainers to participate in the selection of, and conduct the training of, the volunteer PSOs. Ongoing expenses, like out-of-pocket costs of the PSOs, resource materials, and subsequent training should not be that great. The efforts and commitment of the peer supporters are what largely keep the program in operation.

The Selection Process Of Peer Support Officers

Ideally, peer supporters should be representative of their fellow officers. They should represent all ranks, and include men and women as well as different ethnic groups. Even though all ranks should be represented, a peer support program should treat all PSOs equally. One's rank is not relevant in the context of peer support.

It is important that peer supporters be viewed as men and women who genuinely want to help their fellow officers, and not be seen as management or union appointees. Becoming a peer supporter should be for the pure purpose of helping others and not be viewed as a reward or perk.

To solicit PSO volunteers for the program, it can be helpful to place an advertisement in the union newspaper or magazine. It can also be helpful to put flyers in commands. The flyer should include information about the program, and discuss the characteristics that peers should have. In this way, applicants can be initially self-screened to some extent. Among the qualities that are most important in peer supporters are: being gregarious, dependable, mature, sensitive, and compassionate.

It is extremely important to individually interview all applicants. Preferably, the program director and the clinician/trainers should conduct the interviews. Some questions that might be included in the interview are:

1. Tell us about yourself.

2. What motivated you to participate in this program?

3. What previous experiences of yours will be helpful to you as a peer supporter?

4. What personal qualities and characteristics of yours will help you to be an effective peer supporter?

5. Have you ever had an experience, either personal or work-related, where you could have benefited from talking to a peer supporter?

6. Have you had any experience with professional counseling and/or support groups?

7. What are your feelings and attitudes about alcohol, different ethnic and religious groups, and homosexuality?

8. What would your co-workers say your greatest strength is? What would your co-workers say your greatest weakness is?

9. What other commitments do you have in your life that might prevent you from being truly available as a peer supporter?

The purpose of the interview is to find individuals who are open to be being trained in communication techniques that differ significantly from law enforcement training. In addition, it is important for these individuals to be sensitive to the kinds of emotional crises that people experience. It is acceptable, even preferable, to choose candidates who have experienced their own personal crises as long as they have resolved them or are open to resolving them. It is also helpful to choose individuals who demonstrate the willingness and ability to bond with others as a team, and to be open about sharing their thoughts, feelings and experiences in a large training group setting.

In addition to learning about each applicant, another purpose of the interview is to give applicants a clearer picture of the program and the level of commitment expected of them. Applicants need to fully understand the nature of the program in order to be more aware of the role, expectations, requirements, and limitations of peer support. They are then able to make a more informed decision about participating in the program if they are selected. If a person does not have sufficient time to devote to the program, it is better to decline before training commences. Those selected then undergo the extensive training in the topics that have been discussed in Chapters 1 through 6 of this manual.

The actual training combines numerous experiential exercises with this educational material. It is suggested that the initial training be held at a site, such as a residential center, with communal meals and overnight stay, to better promote bonding among the participants.

Such an environment allows for greater openness and trust to develop. As a result, trainees form stronger connections with each other, and better learn to work together as a team.

One of the most beneficial aspects of this training model is the use of role playing exercises. This is best done is groups of three (triads) where one trainee "plays" the client, another "plays" a peer support officer, and the third functions as an observer. The client presents a scenario concerning a particular problem. The PSO attempts to help the client by utilizing the various skills and information that have been provided to that point. After ten to fifteen minutes, the observer reviews what he or she saw, and the PSO and client also share their feelings and observations about the interaction. Roles are rotated until each member of the triad has experienced each of the three roles. Trainees are asked to use their own personal situations whenever possible, and thereby, can experience an additional benefit from these exercises.

For those utilizing this manual who are not in an official training program, it is helpful to create practice role-play situations with fellow officers utilizing the same model discussed above. Examples of relevant scenarios can be found throughout this manual.

Role-playing is an excellent method for practicing techniques before doing the actual work of a PSO. While many trainees complain about doing role-plays because they feel self-conscious practicing in front of others, they are later grateful for the opportunity to learn from their "mistakes" before working with actual clients. These exercises have proven to be very effective in preparing PSOs for the variety of situations that they later encounter.

At the beginning of training, most trainees are anxious about their ability to function successfully as peer supporters. By the end of formalized training, they generally feel more confident and secure that the skills they have acquired will help them when working with clients.

Creating A Mental Health Referral Network

Another crucial element in developing a peer support program is creating a comprehensive referral network of mental health professionals and community resources. Since peer supporters will need to make referrals during the course of their work, having appropriate resources available to them is fundamental. It is also very important that the network consist of clinicians and professional programs that have experience and familiarity with the concerns and problems of law enforcement personnel and their families. In addition to having experience working with officers and family members, some other criteria include the ability to accept the officer's insurance and geographic convenience.

It can be helpful to utilize a clinician coordinator to set up such a network. A questionnaire that contains relevant information needs to be developed and mailed to clinicians. It is also helpful to screen clinicians by phone or in person to get a clearer sense of their interest in and commitment to working with law enforcement families. One source of identifying clinicians, who are sensitive to law enforcement issues, can come from peer supporters who have utilized therapy for their own personal issues.

The Operation of a 24-Hour Help-Line

Most peer support programs operate on the basis of officers voluntarily reaching out for help. Officers can avail themselves of help in several ways. Some officers may solicit help directly from a PSO. However, our experience has shown that most officers requesting assistance do so through a 24-hour help-line. Such a help-line needs to have a PSO assigned at all times, twenty-four hours a day, seven days a week. If it is not feasible to have a 24 hour manned help-line, a beeper system can be utilized as follows:

♦ A person calling the help-line hears a taped message and is asked to leave a name and phone number.

♦ When a message is left, the answering machine sends a message by a beeper to the PSO covering the help-line. It is important to set-up the system so that the PSO returns the call within <u>five</u> minutes of getting beeped. This demonstrates the responsiveness of the program and makes PSOs available for dealing with crisis situations.

♦ Upon returning a phone call, the PSO confirms that the person answering the phone is the person who called the help-line. The PSO then briefly introduces him or herself to the client in the following manner:

"Hello, my name is _____. I am a trained volunteer Peer Support Officer for _____. This is a confidential program. How can I help you?"

♦ It is important that you do not leave a message with another person, or on an answering machine, that identifies you as a peer support officer. This information can breach the caller's confidentiality.

♦ It is generally preferable that peer support officers do not acknowledge or divulge their rank. Give your first name to the client, but do not tell the person your rank or where you work. This information can interfere with the development of trust and openness.

♦ If a caller leaves a message requesting a specific PSO by name, respond to the call, and ascertain the caller's need for assistance. If appropriate, contact the PSO that was requested.

♦ Many callers will ask for a referral to a mental health professional. Experience has shown that it is generally preferable to meet with a client <u>in person</u> before giving a referral. Talking to a client in person provides more information than telephone contact, enables you to provide the most appropriate referral, and allows for a more meaningful interaction to occur.

♦ In those instances where a PSO has a team leader, it is suggested that the PSO confer about help-line calls and referrals.

It is helpful for the peer support program to keep non-identifying statistical data in order to monitor the activities and the effectiveness of the program. Keeping records is also important to provide information to the agency or any outside funding organizations about how the program has been utilized. Funding is often contingent upon substantiating a program's effectiveness.

It is preferable to have all PSOs attend monthly team meetings, to be kept abreast of policies and procedures as well as to discuss specific issues that arise. It is also preferable for all PSOs to have at least one buddy PSO that he or she calls regularly for support. A peer support team needs its individual members to work together in their attempts to help others.

Chapter 8

SOME BASIC QUESTIONS AND ANSWERS

What's the goal of a peer support program?

A peer support program attempts to help officers before their problems grow to crisis proportions. In recent years, many departments have experienced high rates of officers committing suicide. It is preferable for such a program to be separate from the department and be run by the voluntary efforts of trained peers. Officers voluntarily come to the program where they receive confidential help.

Ethical Questions

Is it really important for me to explain the instances where I may have to violate confidentiality?

At first you want to reassure the client of the importance of confidentiality. Address exceptions only when relevant and necessary.

Is it appropriate to accept a drink at a bar from my client?

No. Avoid meeting at a bar. Your work as a PSO is not social. Drinking alcohol distorts one's ability to communicate with a client and should be avoided. A coffee shop is a more appropriate meeting place.

Can I accept a gift from a client?

Many clients will be grateful for your help, and want to give you something in return for the help they have received. Their expression of appreciation is all that you should accept.

Can I meet a client at his/her house or apartment? Do I invite a client to mine?

No. It is important to meet in a neutral setting, such as a coffee shop. Avoid meeting in intimate settings. If that is impossible, you may have to go to someone's home if they, for example, cannot get a babysitter. You may want to bring another PSO along with you. First, ask the client for permission.

What should I do if I feel an attraction to my client?

Dual relationships can harm your client. If you feel an attraction to your client, and you want to pursue a relationship with that client, bear in mind that this is <u>not appropriate.</u> You may need to refer that client to another PSO. Explain your reasons for doing so.

In addition, it is necessary to allow substantial time to pass before establishing a personal relationship with someone that you have worked with as a client. Professional ethical guidelines prescribe that a minimum of two years should elapse before any personal relationship may occur with a former client.

What if I don't like the officer who is asking for my help?

Personality clashes can and do occur. You may not like everyone who seeks your help. It is useful to focus on the <u>problems</u> of the client rather than the personality of the individual. If you find you have a strong negative reaction to someone, refer that person to another PSO. In the meantime, remain as positive and supportive as possible.

What do I do if the client begins to talk about being involved in an illegal act?

Remind the client that there are some legal limits regarding confidentiality in a peer support relationship. At this time, PSOs are not protected by privileged communication. In the rare event of being subpoenaed, a PSO would be legally bound to testify. To avoid this situation, help the client refocus the conversation to his or her feelings rather than his or her illegal actions or behaviors.

Interpersonal Communication Questions

What can I do to build rapport with a client?

Build rapport by relating in a caring, respectful, and accepting way and by utilizing the listening skills you are learning in training.

How can I build rapport with a client who has been drinking?

When under the influence of alcohol, a person's judgment is impaired, and that person is unable to integrate information well. Don't work too hard trying to make a client understand some of the effects of alcohol abuse while the person is inebriated. That person will probably not recall the majority of the conversation anyway. You can make sure, however, that the person is not suicidal and is not in any imminent danger. Contact the person the next day to see if he or she is willing to seek help. At that time, the person may be more receptive to information about alcohol abuse.

How do I know that I've achieved good communication with a client?

Observe the person to whom you're speaking and notice subtle non-verbal cues, such as nodding of the head and eye contact. Ask the client about how he or she <u>feels</u> about the interaction.

I don't think I handled the situation well. I'm concerned I did something wrong.

Second-guessing one's work is natural, and is a good method to improve and refine skills. Remember that no one is perfect. What is most important is that you are there for the client. The procedures you employ can always be adjusted or improved.

Problem Area Questions

How can I help a client know that he or she may be experiencing a problem with alcohol?

Ask a client these questions:

1. Do you drink alcohol?
2. How often do you drink alcohol?
3. How much do you drink?
4. Have you ever experienced blackouts?
5. Have you ever wished there was a time when you didn't drink alcohol?

After asking these questions, you can also ask if a friend or family member ever suggested that the person drinks too much. Another question to ask is if the person is experiencing problems at work or in relationships as a result of drinking alcohol.

I am a PSO in recovery. Is it a good idea for me to break my anonymity with a client?

That's a judgment call for you to make. It is up to you whether you feel comfortable disclosing your personal life. It is not mandatory. With some clients you may feel comfortable sharing a little bit of your personal life in order to help them gain a broader perspective. With others, you may not. Trust your intuition.

What do I do if someone calls the help-line and tells me that he or she is thinking of suicide?

Be sure to take the situation seriously. Go through your checklist of questions assessing suicidal thoughts and plans. Take as much time as necessary to develop rapport and gain a commitment from the person that he or she will not harm him or herself. Remember **PLAID PALS**.

The following is a more detailed response to handling a call from a suicidal person:

1. Try to stay calm. Take a deep breath. Just be yourself and allow your concern and empathy to come through.

2. Use your listening skills. Allow the person to express their feelings of unhappiness, anger, etc. Just by being there and listening you are helping the person to feel better.

3. It is very important to be accepting and non-judgmental, to reinforce the caller's having reached out for help.

4. If the caller is hinting at having suicidal thoughts, ask the question, "Are you thinking of hurting or killing yourself?" By doing so you demonstrate your concern, and that you are taking the caller's situation seriously.

5. If the caller is having suicidal thoughts, remember to ask your questions concerning a plan, available means, other previous attempts, etc.

6. By having the contact with you, and experiencing your care and interest, most suicidal callers will become less agitated and better able to get through the crisis.

7. Be careful not to minimize the caller's concerns or attempt to quickly provide a solution to their problem. Remember that it is the person's pain and feelings that are of importance during this call.

8. Check out whether the person is intoxicated and whether the person is in need of immediate medical attention.

9. Remember that as a PSO you do not have to deal with situations alone. You can ask for help, if possible, during

the call, and can certainly reach out to other PSOs afterwards.

10.   The caller may initially say that he or she is calling about someone else who is suicidal, and ask what to do to help this friend. After speaking to the person for a while, if you suspect that the caller may be the suicidal person, you might ask whether the caller has ever had suicidal thoughts.

What do I do when a client requests to be hospitalized?

First of all, don't panic. Tell the person you will meet with him or her. If the client believes it is an absolute emergency, he/she can go to the nearest emergency room for immediate hospitalization. When you meet with the client, explore the reasons the client wants to be hospitalized, and evaluate for yourself if you think it is an appropriate decision. Frequently, hospitalization is not the best option. Seeing a therapist is often preferable.

Self-Care

I'm feeling overwhelmed by the PSO work. What should I do?

Talk to your buddy and team coordinator as a way to relieve some of the stress. If necessary, arrange with your team coordinator to take some time off from PSO work.

Operational Questions

What do I do if a supervisor or other third party comes to me and tells me an officer needs help?

It is preferable that the peer support program be set up in such a way that in order for someone to get help, he or she must seek it out directly. If this is the case in your program, you can tell your boss that your peer support program is voluntary, and that he or she can encourage the person to come and talk to you, mentioning that your program is confidential and independent of the department. You might also mention that you are not at liberty to discuss whether the person comes to you for help since that would be a breach of confidentiality.

What do I do if someone comes to me for help that is already in trouble with the department? Some examples may include:

A. **A supervisor has removed weapons, either officially or unofficially**

B. **Disciplinary charges or criminal charges have occurred**

C. **Disciplinary charges, such as from a domestic violence allegation, <u>may</u> occur**

It is the policy of certain peer support programs that once the department is involved, the program cannot provide any services to the officer. However, you can refer the officer to a union delegate for help or for outside help of some sort.

If I get a help-line call from an angry client, should I get another PSO to go with me?

If you feel unsafe, absolutely bring along another PSO. He or she can wait in the car for you or sit at another table in the coffee shop. You might ask the client for permission to have the other PSO join the conversation if you believe it would be helpful.

What do I do if I'm manning the help-line, and the caller is of the opposite sex from me and has marital problems? Is it problematic to help someone in this situation?

It may be problematic to work with someone of the opposite sex who has marital problems. Ask the client if he or she would prefer to work with a PSO of the same gender.

Can a client bring a spouse or romantic partner to see me?

No, that poses a problem for confidentiality. If a client feels more comfortable coming with his/her partner, suggest that the partner sit in the car or at a different table in the restaurant.

How are firearms safeguarded?

It is important for the program to have procedures to safeguard firearms that maintain the confidentiality of the client. This is an area where advance planning is required. The program coordinator and the department must address this issue jointly.

HELPFUL HINTS

The following questions and comments are suggestions that you may find useful when talking to a client. Please feel free to expand on them to make them sound more authentic for you.

Introductory Comments

"What brings you here to talk to me?"

"How can I help you?"

"What can I do for you?"

"How do you feel about coming to talk to me?"

Open Ended Questions

"How did that experience make you feel?"

"What has been going on in your relationship?"

"How are you doing right now?"

"What motivated you to do that?"

Empathic Comments

"I imagine that you are feeling sad (or upset, confused, disappointed, etc.)"

"I understand how you feel. I'd feel the same way."

"That sounds like a very difficult situation for you to be going through right now."

"I can see how much you've been affected by this experience."

Reflection of Feelings Comments

"I can see how upsetting this is for you right now."

"You seem really angry about that."

"You seem to have a lot of feelings about this."

Summary Comments

"What I hear you saying is . . ."

"I understand that . . ."

"Let me see if I fully understand what you're saying."

GLOSSARY

Blackouts - inability to recall an event while under the influence of alcohol.

Burnout – a syndrome of emotional exhaustion that occurs when one over-works as a helper with troubled individuals. It is also referred to as compassion fatigue.

Confidentiality – an ethical principle of protecting and respecting the privacy of the individual who is seeking your help.

Denial – a psychological defense mechanism that prevents an individual from recognizing self-destructive behavior.

Dual relationship - a situation where one takes on a second role with a client that may lead to a conflict of interest and therefore undermines the PSO-client relationship.

Empathy – a process of imagining oneself in the circumstances of a client without judging or evaluating the behavior or feelings of the client.

Enabling – contributing to a significant other's destructive behavior by shielding him or her from negative consequences.

Hypervigilance – interpreting the environment around you as always being potentially life-threatening and dangerous. It is also referred to as "seeing through cop's eyes."

Open-ended Questions – questions that solicit information from clients and allow them to explore further and elaborate more fully their concerns and feelings.

Paraphrasing –restating the thoughts or meaning of what a client has said.

Peer Support – a process whereby trained colleagues provide assistance to coworkers through listening, understanding, and providing appropriate referrals when necessary.

PSO – a law enforcement officer who has been trained to provide peer support to coworkers.

PLAID PALS – a memory device for assessing suicidal risk.

Stonewalling – a destructive communication pattern that occurs when someone stops responding, withdraws, and is silent, conveying disapproval, icy distance, and smugness.

12-Step Programs – Support groups modeled on, and including, Alcoholics Anonymous, to help individuals abstain from addictions and further their personal development.

REFERENCES

Cummings, James P.; "Police Stress and the Suicide Link." The Police Chief, October 1996, 84-95.

Danto, B. I.; "Police Suicide." Police Stress, 1, 32-35, 1978.

Fishkin, Gerald Loren; *Police Burnout: Signs, Symptoms, and Solutions.* Harcourt Brace Jovanovich: New York, 1987.

Gottman, John; *Why Marriages Succeed or Fail . . And How You Can Make Yours Last.* Simon & Schuster: New York, 1994.

Janik, J; "Who Needs Peer Support?" The Police Chief, January 1995, 38-41.

Janik, J. & Kravitz, H.M.; "Linking work and domestic problems with police suicide." Suicide & Life-threatening Behavior. 24:267-74, 1994.

Johnson, Leanor Boulin; "Testimony of Work-Family Stress among Police Officers: An Empirical Study." Submitted to U.S. House of Representatives Select Committee on Children, Youth, and Families. Washington, D.C., 1991.

Kirschman, Ellen; *I Love a Cop: What Police Families Need to Know.* The Guilford Press: New York, 1997.

Maslach, Christina; *Burnout-The Cost of Caring.* Prentice-Hall, Inc.: New Jersey, 1982.

Myrick, Robert and Sorenson, Don; *Peer Helping: A Practical Guide* (Second Edition). Educational Media Corporation: Minneapolis, 1997.

Ryan, Andrew H.; "Afternburn: The Victimization of Police Families." The Police Chief, October 1997, 63-67.

Violanti, J.M.; "The Mystery Within: Understanding Police Suicide," FBI Law Enforcement Bulletin, February 1995, 19-23.

APPENDIX

Training NYPD Police Officers as Peer Supporters

For the past four years, The Peer Support Training Institute, a division of Manhattan Counseling and Psychotherapy Associates (MCPA), LLC, has trained fifty New York City police officers a year to become peer supporters. Training has been completed for the fourth group of peer support officers (PSOs) who are a part of the Members Assistance Program (MAP). These men and women are New York City police officers who volunteer their services to help fellow police officers in need of emotional support. The training, both academic and experiential, covers a wide-range of topics and provides the peer support officers with vital information needed when working with clients.

Peer support programs are very effective in helping officers to more effectively deal with stress and emotional difficulties. Empirical research has shown that police officers are more likely to talk about their problems to a fellow officer than to anyone else. In the past, many law enforcement personnel have been unwilling to utilize the psychological services of their departments for fear of being stigmatized and for fear of having their career goals disrupted or destroyed. Many have also been unwilling to go to mental health professionals for help because they believed they would not be understood by anyone outside the field of law enforcement. The unwillingness to utilize department services as well as outside services has meant that many officers have not received the help that they needed. This was exemplified by the high suicide rate in 1994 and 1995 within the NYC Police Department. It was evident that the personal problems of certain officers were being left unaddressed. Tragic consequences resulted. Clearly, something needed to be done to help NYC police officers.

To provide this help, The Members Assistance Program was initiated by Mr. William Genet, a Citywide Trustee of the NYC Patrolmen's Benevolent Association (PBA). MAP is a voluntary, union-sponsored program that is supported by but independent of the NYC police department. The help that police officers receive is strictly confidential; no departmental records are kept. The goal of MAP is to change the belief that many police officers hold that seeking help is a sign of weakness rather than a sign of strength. MAP received funding from the New York City Council to train fifty police officers a year to become peer supporters, with the eventual goal that two hundred officers would be trained to provide services to the 40,000 police officers of New York City.

The Peer Support Training Institute of MCPA was hired to provide the training. The staff of MCPA consists of licensed mental health practitioners who have had many years of experience working with police officers and their family members. The training, tailored to the specific needs of the New York City Police Department, follows the guidelines recommended by the Psychological Services Section of the International Chiefs of Police. Training consists of eighty intensive hours, providing officers with various skills, including interpersonal communication techniques as well as assessment and referral information.

The director of MAP and The Peer Support Training Institute clinicians interview all volunteers before they are accepted to the program. Each person is asked a series of questions about personal characteristics and experiences that are relevant to being a peer support officer. Candidates are also asked about their ability to volunteer their time and energy to MAP. During the interview, the responsibilities they will be expected to assume once they become peer supporters are discussed.

Training combines both experiential exercises and educational information. The first three days of training are held at a residential center to promote bonding among the participants. Peer supporters are not immune from experiencing the stressors of every day life and from having emotional problems, and it is vital that they learn how to reach out to each other for support when it is needed. Each training group is limited of twenty-five officers in order to facilitate their getting to know each other more easily. The program's success is dependent upon participants opening up and trusting each other, and to later serve as role models for their clients.

One of the primary goals of training is for the PSOs to develop greater sensitivity and empathy for others. Through a series of experiential exercises that focus on examining one's own experiences and feelings, trainees become more aware of their own issues, emotions, assumptions, and judgments. This helps them become more understanding of and compassionate to others. They learn the importance of confidentiality and being non-judgmental in getting clients to trust them. They are also made aware of other ethical issues, such as appropriate boundaries and avoiding dual relationships with clients.

The trainees are introduced to the role and purpose of being a peer support officer. They are to be available as a supportive resource for fellow officers, utilizing helping skills and concepts to assist others. They are to be a friendly sounding board to allow clients to explore ideas, feelings, and alternatives to situations. They are not to give advice or solve a client's problems. As police officers, the trainees have been taught to communicate and interact in a certain way with the public. While this is effective in their duties on the job, it is not the best communication style as a peer supporter. PSO training teaches them alternate communication techniques and demonstrates the importance of listening to and acknowledging a fellow officer's problems rather than giving advice and solving the person's problems.

Interpersonal communication topics such as listening, relating, and responding skills are covered. Training is reinforced by role-play exercises where trainees rotate playing the roles of a peer supporter and a client portraying a particular problem. Role-play exercises are effective preparation for the work peer supporters will eventually be doing. They are also instructed how to man the 24-hour help-line of MAP, which has become the primary way troubled officers seek help from this program.

The unique stressors of police work and some of the resultant problems that can occur are discussed along with stress-management techniques. Trainees are provided with information about the signs and symptoms of depression and suicide as well as information about relationship issues and alcohol problems. They are also taught how to recognize critical incident stress and post-traumatic stress disorder. While peer supporters do not provide counseling to others, they do need to be able to identify certain symptoms and behaviors in order to make appropriate referrals.

One of the primary goals in establishing a peer support program was to reduce the number of suicides committed by NYC police officers. Approximately fifteen suicides have been prevented during the first three years of the program's existence. Another goal of MAP has been to encourage officers to seek help before a crisis occurs. Approximately 1000 individuals have called MAP's help-line for assistance. At least half of the callers have met with a peer supporter in person and have been referred to a mental health clinician.

At the beginning of training, most trainees are anxious about their abilities to function successfully as peer supporters. By the end of formalized training, they feel more confident and secure that the skills they have acquired will help them when working with clients. Before servicing the help-line alone, they are apprenticed with an experienced PSO mentor who helps guide them through the ropes. They also are required to attend monthly meetings, a forum where their skills are further refined. They also know that they are not alone, and they are strongly encouraged to reach out to other peer supporters for help when needed.

Training these dedicated men and women has been a most rewarding experience for us, and one that we hope to continue in our quest to help police officers deal more effectively with the stress of their jobs.

About the Authors

Rachelle Katz, Ed.D., is a licensed marriage and family therapist and psychotherapist in private practice with specialties in eating disorders, alcoholism counseling, and relationship counseling. She is a Certified Addictions Specialist in both alcoholism and substance abuse. Dr. Katz is a clinical member of the American Association for Family Therapy, the American Psychological Association, and the American Counseling Association. She served as an honorary Police Surgeon with the New York City Transit Police Department from 1990 to 1996.

Ronnie M. Hirsh, Ph.D., is a licensed marriage and family therapist and psychotherapist in private practice. He is a Clinical Member of the American Association for Marriage and Family Therapy, Board Certified as a Mental Health Counselor, a Master Addictions Counselor, Certified Employee Assistance Professional and a Certified and Approved Consultant in Clinical Hypnosis of the American Society of Clinical Hypnosis. In addition, he is a full member of ASLET, The American Society of Law Enforcement Trainers. His specialties include hypnosis, alcoholism counseling, relationship counseling (couples and families), as well as individual psychotherapy. He is a former educator, and served as a

Police Surgeon (Hon) with the New York City Transit Police Department from 1990 to 1996.

 **Daniel I. Cohen, Ph.D.** is a licensed psychologist with a private psychotherapy practice. He is trained and certified in Gestalt Therapy and is a member of the American Psychological Association, the New York State Psychological Association, and the Association for Humanistic Psychology. Dr. Cohen has over twenty-five years of experience in private practice working with individuals, couples and families. For the past 4 1/2 years he has been actively involved in the training of police officers as peer supporters. In his practice, he has worked extensively with police officers and their families.

NOTES

NOTES

NOTES

NOTES

NOTES

NOTES

NOTES

NOTES

NOTES

NOTES

NOTES

BOOK ORDER INFORMATION

Cop to Cop:
A Peer Support Training Manual for Law Enforcement Officers (2nd Edition)

(222 pages, Paperback ISBN 0-9669496-3-3) is available as a comprehensive training manual suitable as a textbook for law enforcement personnel seeking to learn how to render effective peer support. It is best used as part of a formal training program but can be used as a self-instruction tool.

List Price:$40.00

Cop to Cop: A Pocket Handbook for Peer Support Officers.

(104 pages, Paperback ISBN 0-9669496-2-5) is a companion pocket-sized summary of the basics of peer support.

List price $15.00

PEER SUPPORT TRAINING INSTITUTE

books may be ordered by calling

(212) 477-8050

or by using the order form on our web site

www.peersupport.com